The Great Gatsby

F. SCOTT FITZGERALD

Level 5

Retold by Celia Turvey
Series Editors: Andy Hopkins and Jocelyn Potter

Pearson Education Limited
Edinburgh Gate, Harlow,
Essex CM20 2JE, England
and Associated Companies throughout the world.

ISBN: 978-1-4058-6517-3

First published in the Longman Fiction Series 1993
This adaptation first published in 1996
First published by Penguin Books 2000
This edition published 2008

1 3 5 7 9 10 8 6 4 2

Text copyright © Penguin Books Ltd 2000
This edition copyright © Pearson Education Ltd 2008

Typeset by Graphicraft Ltd, Hong Kong
Set in 11/14pt Bembo
Printed in China
SWTC/01

Published by Pearson Education Ltd in association with
Penguin Books Ltd, both companies being subsidiaries of Pearson Plc

For a complete list of the titles available in the Penguin Readers series please write to your local
Pearson Longman office or to: Penguin Readers Marketing Department, Pearson Education,
Edinburgh Gate, Harlow, Essex CM20 2JE, England.

Contents

Introduction

'They're no good, any of them!' I shouted across the lawn, and I meant Tom and Daisy, and all of Gatsby's fashionable 'friends'. 'You're worth the whole lot of them!'

What is any man or woman worth? That is a question that some of the characters in *The Great Gatsby* struggle with and others simply ignore.

At the beginning of the novel Jay Gatsby is a mysterious character. No one knows where he has come from, how he has made his fortune or why he has bought an expensive house in West Egg on Long Island. But *everyone* seems to appear every weekend at the brilliant parties at his grand house.

Nick Carraway is the storyteller and he connects East and West Egg for us. He is Gatsby's neighbour, and he knows Tom and Daisy Buchanan from East Egg, the most fashionable place to live on Long Island. Nick himself comes from a wealthy Midwestern family and looks at life on the east coast through the eyes of an outsider. His description of two very different worlds coming together gives us an idea of what life was like in the United States in the 1920s.

But why are these two worlds thrown together? The Buchanans have little interest in anyone outside their circle of rich, fashionable friends; *they* do not attend Gatsby's parties. But Gatsby is in West Egg for a purpose which involves the Buchanans. He has come to Long Island to find Daisy and to claim her.

About five years earlier, Gatsby and Daisy had a love affair, but Gatsby did not have enough to offer a girl like Daisy. They went their separate ways, and Gatsby worked hard to change himself into the kind of man that Daisy's world could accept. Now he has come to find her, to tell her that he loves her and to take her away with him.

Will Gatsby's dream come true? Will Daisy leave Tom and give up everything she has to be with Gatsby? Will the two worlds come together through them?

Francis Scott Key Fitzgerald was born in Minnesota in 1896. The two different sides of his family helped to shape him into the kind of writer he became. Like many of the characters in *The Great Gatsby*, his father, Edward, came from a wealthy upper-class family. In fact, Mr Fitzgerald named his son after a distant cousin, Francis Scott Key, the man who wrote 'The Star-Spangled Banner' the national song, showing by this that the Fitzgeralds came from traditional, American roots. In contrast to the highly respected Fitzgeralds, Francis Scott's mother, Mollie McQuillan, came from a family of poor Irish farmers, but in the US her father, like the Great Gatsby himself, achieved the American Dream and, through hard work, became a wealthy shop owner.

When his own business failed in 1908, Edward Fitzgerald moved his family back to Minnesota and lived on the money that Mollie's father had left her. F. Scott Fitzgerald understood the advantages of an upper-class background as well as the advantages of having a lot of money, even if it had to be earned. In his writing, especially in *The Great Gatsby*, he tries to answer the question of what actually defines a person.

By the time he entered Princeton University in 1913, the young Fitzgerald already knew that he wanted to be a writer. He was well suited for this profession because, as he said himself, he had a strongly romantic imagination and was very sensitive to the promises of life. He was a leading member of a group of Princeton students who were interested in literature, art and the theatre. Unfortunately, he wrote plays and short stories instead of studying for exams. He left Princeton without his degree in 1917, and joined the army for the last two years of the World War

I. Believing that he would die in battle, Fitzgerald quickly wrote his first novel.

In June 1918, the army sent Fitzgerald to Alabama, and he fell deeply in love with eighteen-year-old Zelda Sayre. The love between Fitzgerald and Zelda shaped their lives and eventually damaged both of them. But in 1918, Zelda refused to marry Fitzgerald because he had no money.

Fitzgerald went to New York, but after failing to make his fortune he returned to Minnesota and re-wrote his novel. *This Side of Paradise*, about a young man's search for financial success and romantic happiness, came out in 1920 and was immediately successful.

The novel made Fitzgerald rich and famous. His short stories soon appeared in the most fashionable magazines as well as in more serious ones. He was then able to marry Zelda, and the couple became known as the prince and princess of high society, according to the celebrated journalist and novelist Ring Lardner.

The Fitzgeralds were the most beautiful and most fashionable American couple of the 1920s. Their lifestyle defined the age they lived in. They spent money freely, ate in the best restaurants, went to the best parties, and danced and drank until dawn. Then Fitzgerald wrote about it all. His second novel, *The Beautiful and the Damned*, tells the story of a handsome young man and his beautiful wife and how their lives end in disaster.

To avoid his own path to personal disaster and to concentrate more on his writing and less on his lifestyle, Fitzgerald took Zelda and their three-year-old daughter to France in 1924. Fitzgerald was criticized at that time for his heavy drinking. Although he insisted that he never drank when he was writing, Fitzgerald's alcoholism and Zelda's habit of drinking heavily led to frequent quarrels between the couple. However, Fitzgerald managed to write *The Great Gatsby* during this period, and the novel appeared in April 1925. The story was praised, but the book, which is based on Fitzgerald's own divided nature, was financially disappointing.

The Fitzgeralds stayed in France until the end of 1926 and became friends with writers like Ernest Hemingway. But the period was marked more by Zelda's failing mental health than by F. Scott Fitzgerald's writing. He made very little progress on his fourth novel, and they returned to the US to escape their exciting, but expensive, life in France.

Fitzgerald's writing still did not go well and the family returned to France in 1929, where Zelda worked hard to begin a career as a professional dancer, although she was already twenty-nine years old. The difficult training further damaged her health.

Through the 1930s, the Fitzgeralds fought an unsuccessful battle to save their marriage. At the same time, Fitzgerald struggled with his writing, only finishing his next novel, *Tender is the Night*, in 1934. Zelda's mental health became worse, and she spent the rest of her life in and out of mental hospitals.

Between 1936 and 1937, Fitzgerald was ill, drunk and unable to make much money. He lived in cheap hotels in North Carolina to be near Zelda's hospital and kept in contact with his daughter mostly by post.

He went to Hollywood in 1937 and began writing for films. His salary was good enough to pay Zelda's hospital bills, but never enough to pay for his drink and his lifestyle. He fell in love again, and spent his last few years with a film journalist called Sheilah Graham, who accepted his drunken nights and made a home for him. He began his Hollywood novel, *The Last Tycoon*, in 1939 but died of a heart attack in Graham's apartment on December 21, 1940 before he could finish it. Zelda's life ended in a fire at a mental hospital in 1948.

F. Scott Fitzgerald died believing that he was a failure, at life and at writing. At the time of his death, he was not an important name in American literature. But since 1960 he has been considered one of America's greatest and most original writers.

For many students of literature, *The Great Gatsby*, with its examination of the American character, defines what an American novel should be. But Fitzgerald is not only remembered for his writing. Gatsby's rich, fashionable world with beautiful people, amazing houses and exciting parties mirrored Fitzgerald's life with Zelda in Paris and in the United States. Their brilliant, but eventually disastrous, lifestyle provided the heart of Fitzgerald's short stories and novels and has become an important part of American history. If you want to understand the spirit of the 1920s and 30s, while looking underneath the extraordinary appearance of life in those days, Fitzgerald's work is a good place to start.

The Great Gatsby is one of a group of novels that came out of the United States after World War I and gave the world an idea of what Americans were really like. Many critics consider *Gatsby* to be about the American Dream, the optimistic belief that no matter what background you come from, if you work hard enough, you can get rich, find love and happiness, and even become president.

But Fitzgerald and other writers in his group questioned this picture of the US and also began to question the meaning of life itself. The Great War had not solved the world's problems; instead, countries everywhere faced enormous financial difficulties and individuals began to wonder how to deal with the new century.

The novel leaves us with some important questions. What is success? What is love? What makes a person human, admirable, truly wealthy? These questions and the warnings they give us about life guarantee *The Great Gatsby* a place in American literature. Today the novel is taught in high schools and universities across the US and around the world, and four films and a play have been made from the story.

Chapter 1   West Egg and East Egg

Last autumn, after only six months in New York, I came back to this midwestern city where I grew up. There have been Carraways living here for seventy years: the first one was my grandfather's brother, who came here in 1851 and started the business that my father carries on today. I never saw this great-uncle, but I'm supposed to look like him.

I finished my studies at New Haven University in 1915, just a quarter of a century after my father, and a little later I went over to Europe to take part in the Great War. I liked Europe so much that I came back to the United States feeling restless. Instead of being the warm centre of the world, the Middle West now seemed like its rough edge. So I decided to go East and learn the bond business. Everybody I knew was in the bond business, so I supposed it could support one more single man. Father agreed to pay my living costs for a year, and after various delays I came East in the spring of 1922 – for ever, I thought.

I intended to find rooms in New York City, but it was the beginning of summer and I had just left a country of green lawns and friendly trees, so when a young man at the office suggested that we take a house together in the country, it sounded like a great idea. He found a small house to rent at only eighty dollars a month. But at the last minute the firm ordered him to Washington and I went out to the country alone. A Finnish woman from the village came in to make my bed and cook my breakfast. It was lonely for a few days until one morning some man, more recently arrived than I, stopped me on the road.

'How do you get to West Egg village?' he asked helplessly.

I told him. And as I walked on, I was lonely no longer. I was not a newcomer any more, I was a guide, a pathfinder.

And so with the sunshine and the great bursts of leaves growing on the trees, I had the feeling that life was beginning over again with the summer.

There was so much to read, for one thing. I bought a lot of books about banking and money matters, and they stood on my shelf in red and gold, promising to unfold the shining secrets of wealth. And I had the intention of reading many other books besides. When I was at college I was interested in literature, and now I was going to bring back all such things into my life.

By chance I had rented a house in one of the strangest societies in North America. It was on Long Island, which stretches more than sixty miles east of New York. Between Long Island and the mainland lies a narrow part of the sea called Long Island Sound. On the coast, twenty miles from the city, there are two unusual formations of land, almost exactly egg-shaped. They stick out into the Sound like a pair of great eggs, separated by a small bay. But though they are so similar in shape and size, they are quite different in other ways.

I lived at West Egg, the less fashionable of the two. My little house was near the sea, between two enormous houses. The one on my right was very grand by any standard. It was a copy of some French town hall, with a tower on one side, a beautiful swimming pool and a large area of lawns and garden. I knew that a gentleman called Mr Gatsby lived there. My own house was small and ugly, but I had a view of the water, a view of part of my neighbour's lawn, and the comforting nearness of wealthy people – all for eighty dollars a month.

Across the bay the white palaces of fashionable East Egg shone along the water. The history of the summer really begins on the day I drove over there to have dinner with Tom and Daisy Buchanan. Daisy was a distant relative of mine, and I'd known Tom in college. And just after the war I spent two days with them in Chicago.

Tom was one of the most powerful football players there had ever been at New Haven University. His family were extremely wealthy. Now he'd left Chicago and come East, bringing his polo horses with him. It was hard to realize that a man of my own age was wealthy enough to do that.

I don't know why they came East. They had spent a year in France for no special reason, and then wandered here and there, wherever people played polo and were rich together. This time they were going to stay, said Daisy over the telephone, but I didn't believe it. I felt that Tom would keep moving on, as if for ever searching for the excitement of some long-lost football game.

And so it happened that on a warm and windy evening I drove over to East Egg to see two friends I hardly knew. Their house was even grander than I had expected, a large nineteenth-century house looking out over the bay. The lawn started where the sand ended and ran all the way up to the front door. Along the front of the house was a line of tall windows, wide open now to the warm wind. Tom Buchanan, in riding clothes, was standing with his legs apart on the front porch.

He had changed since his New Haven years. Now he was a strongly built man of thirty, with a rather hard mouth and a scornful manner. His riding clothes could not hide the great strength of that body – you could see the muscles moving when his shoulder moved under his thin coat. It was a body of great power – a cruel body.

The rough quality of his speaking voice added to the effect of bad temper which he gave. There were men at New Haven who hated him. He and I had never been close friends, but I always had the feeling that he approved of me and wanted me to like him.

We talked for a few minutes on the sunny porch.

'I've got a nice place here,' he said. Turning me around by one arm, he pointed a wide, flat hand at the lawns, the rose gardens and the motorboat tied up on the beach.

'I bought it from Demaine, the oil man.' He turned me around again suddenly. 'We'll go inside.'

We walked through a high hallway into a bright rosy-coloured room, with long windows at each end. The windows were open and shining white against the fresh grass outside. A wind blew through the room, blowing curtains in at one end and out at the other like pale flags, and then it moved over the wine-coloured floor, making a shadow on it as wind does on the sea.

The only completely still object in the room was an enormous sofa on which two young women were lying. They were both in white, and their dresses were moving in the wind as if they had just been blown into the room after a short flight around the house. I stood there for a moment listening to the curtains blowing. Then Tom shut the back windows and the curtains and the two young women became still.

The younger of the two was a stranger to me. She was stretched out full-length at her end of the sofa, and she didn't move at all when I came in. If she saw me out of the corner of her eyes she gave no sign of it.

The other girl, Daisy, made an attempt to rise. Then she laughed, a lovely little laugh, and I laughed too and came forward into the room.

'I'm too, too happy to see you.' She laughed again, as if she had said something very funny, and held my hand for a moment, looking up into my face as if there was no one in the world she so much wanted to see. That was a way she had. She told me in a soft voice that the name of the other girl was Baker.

Now Miss Baker's lips moved a little, and she bent her head very slightly in my direction.

My relative began to ask me questions in her low, exciting voice. Her face was sad and lovely with bright eyes and a beautiful mouth, but it was the excitement in her voice that men found most difficult to forget.

I told her how I had stopped off in Chicago for a day on my way East, and how a lot of people there had asked me to give her their love.

'Do they miss me?' she cried happily.

'The whole town is sad. All the cars have one wheel painted black.'

'How wonderful! Let's go back, Tom. Tomorrow!' Then she added to me, 'You ought to see the baby.'

'I'd like to.'

'She's asleep. She's three years old. Haven't you ever seen her?'

'Never.'

'Well. You ought to see her. She's–'

Tom Buchanan, who had been moving restlessly around the room, stopped and placed his hand on my shoulder.

'What are you doing at the moment, Nick?'

'I sell bonds.'

'Who do you work for?'

I told him.

'Never heard of them,' he said firmly.

This annoyed me. 'You will hear of them,' I answered.

At this point Miss Baker suddenly came to life, and stood up. 'I'm stiff,' she complained. 'I've been lying on that sofa for as long as I can remember.'

'Don't blame me,' Daisy said. 'I've been trying to get you to New York all afternoon.'

The butler brought in some drinks, and offered them to us.

'No, thanks,' said Miss Baker. 'I'm in training.'

Tom looked at her in disbelief. 'You are?' He drank down his drink as if it were a drop in the bottom of the glass. 'I don't understand how you ever get anything done.'

I looked at Miss Baker, wondering what it was she 'got done'. I enjoyed looking at her. Her grey eyes looked back at me with polite interest out of a pale, interesting face. I realized now that I had seen her, or a picture of her, somewhere before.

'You live in West Egg,' she said. 'I know somebody there.'

'I don't know a single—'

'You must know Gatsby.'

Before I could reply that he was my neighbour, the butler came in to tell us that dinner was ready. Tom put his hand under my arm and moved me from the room.

The two young women went out before us onto a rosy-coloured porch, open towards the sunset, where a table was laid for dinner. There was less wind now.

'In two weeks it'll be the longest day in the year,' said Daisy. She looked at us all brightly. 'Do you always watch for the longest day of the year and then miss it? I always watch for the longest day of the year and then miss it.'

'We ought to plan something,' said Miss Baker in a tired voice, sitting down at the table as if she were getting into bed. She and Daisy talked together, in a manner that was as cool as their white dresses. They were here, and they accepted Tom and me, making only a polite effort to entertain or to be entertained. They knew that soon dinner would be over and a little later the evening too would be over and carelessly put away. It was sharply different from the West, where an evening was hurried through its various stages.

'You make me feel uncivilized, Daisy,' I admitted. 'Can't you talk about crops or something?'

This remark had a strange effect on Tom.

'Civilization is breaking down!' he burst out. 'Have you read *The Rise of the Coloured Empires?*'

'Why, no,' I answered, surprised.

'Well, it's a fine book, and everybody ought to read it. It says that if we don't look out the white race will be pushed under by the coloured races.'

'Tom's getting very serious,' said Daisy. 'He reads deep books with long words in them.'

'Well, these books are all scientific,' said Tom. 'This person has worked out the whole thing. Our race has produced all the things that make up civilization – oh, science and art and all that. And if we don't watch out, these other races will take control of things. Do you see?'

At this moment the telephone rang and the butler went to answer it. He came back and said something close to Tom's ear. Tom looked annoyed, and without a word he went inside.

Daisy leaned forward.

'I love to see you at my table, Nick. You remind me of a – of a rose. Doesn't he?' She turned to Miss Baker.

This was untrue. I am not even a little like a rose. She was saying the first thing that came into her head – but a warmth flowed from her, and her voice was exciting. Then suddenly she excused herself and went into the house.

Miss Baker and I looked at each other. I was about to speak when she sat up and said, 'Ssshh!' We could hear Tom talking on the telephone inside, but we couldn't hear what he was saying. Miss Baker leaned forward, trying to hear. Then the voice stopped.

'This Mr Gatsby you spoke of is my neighbour–' I began.

'Don't talk. I want to hear what happens.'

'Is something happening?' I inquired.

'You mean to say you don't know?' said Miss Baker. 'I thought everybody knew.'

'I don't.'

'Why – Tom's got some woman in New York.'

'Got some woman?' I repeated stupidly.

'Yes. She shouldn't telephone him at dinner time, though.'

Almost before I had understood her meaning, Tom and Daisy were back at the table. I avoided looking at their eyes.

7

A few minutes later we got up from the table, and Tom and Miss Baker wandered inside. I followed Daisy to the front porch, where we sat down.

Daisy looked out into the darkening garden.

'We don't know each other very well, Nick,' she said. 'Even if we are relatives. You didn't come to my wedding.'

'I wasn't back from the war.'

'That's true.' She paused. 'Well, I've had a very bad time, Nick, and I feel pretty hopeless about everything.'

Obviously she had reason to be. I waited, but she didn't say any more. I began rather weakly to question her about her daughter.

'I suppose she talks, and – eats, and everything.'

'Oh, yes.' She looked at me. 'Listen, Nick: let me tell you what I said when she was born. Would you like to hear?'

'Very much.'

'It'll show you how I feel about – things. Well, I asked the nurse right away if it was a boy or a girl. She told me it was a girl, and so I turned my head away and cried. "All right," I said, "I'm glad it's a girl. And I hope she'll be a fool – that's the best thing a girl can be in this world, a beautiful little fool."'

'You see, I think everything's terrible,' she went on. 'Everybody thinks so – the cleverest people. And I *know*. I've been everywhere and seen everything and done everything.'

As soon as her voice stopped, I felt the basic insincerity of what she had said. It worried me. I waited and, sure enough, in a moment she looked at me with a smile of satisfaction on her lovely face – she was pleased to think that she and Tom belonged to this small group of 'clever people' who knew so much about the ways of the world.

♦

Inside, the rose-red room was full of light. Tom and Miss Baker sat at either end of the long sofa, and she read out loud to him

8

from the *Saturday Evening Post*. When we came in she stopped reading and stood up.

'Ten o'clock,' she said. 'Time for this good girl to go to bed.'

'Jordan's going to play in the match tomorrow,' explained Daisy, 'over at Westchester.'

'Oh – you're *Jordan* Baker.'

I knew now why her face was familiar – she was a well-known golf player. Her face had looked out at me from many photographs of the sporting life at Hot Springs and Palm Beach. I had heard some story about her too, an unpleasant story, but I had forgotten what it was.

'Good night,' she said. 'Wake me at eight, won't you.'

'If you'll get up.'

'I will. Good night, Mr Carraway. See you soon.' She went up the stairs.

'Of course you will,' said Daisy. 'In fact I think I'll arrange a marriage. Come over often, Nick, and I'll sort of – oh, throw you together.'

'She's a nice girl,' said Tom after a moment. 'They oughtn't to let her run around the country this way.'

'Who oughtn't to?' inquired Daisy coldly.

'Her family.'

'Her family is one aunt about a thousand years old. Besides, Nick's going to look after her, aren't you, Nick? She's going to spend lots of weekends out here this summer.'

'Is she from New York?' I asked.

'From Louisville, my home town. We were girls together.'

A few minutes later I got up to go home. They came to the door with me and stood side by side in a cheerful square of light. As I started my motor, Daisy called: 'Wait! I forgot to ask you something. We heard you were engaged to marry a girl out West.'

'That's right,' Tom agreed. 'We heard that you were engaged.'

'It's not true. I'm too poor.'

'But we heard it,' Daisy repeated. 'We heard it from three people, so it must be true.'

Of course I knew what they were talking about. The fact that people were saying I was engaged was one of the reasons I had come East. You can't stop going with an old friend because people are talking, and on the other hand I had no intention of being talked into marriage.

Their interest rather touched me. But as I drove away I felt confused about Daisy and Tom, and a little disgusted. It seemed to me that the thing for Daisy to do in this situation was to rush out of the house with her child in her arms. As for Tom, the fact that he 'had some woman in New York' was really less surprising than that he had been upset by a book. He had never been concerned with the world of books and ideas, and didn't know how to deal with them.

When I reached my house in West Egg, I put the car in the garage and sat for a while in the yard. The wind had dropped, leaving a bright, moonlit night. The dark shape of a moving cat wandered across the moonlight, and, turning my head to watch it, I saw that I was not alone. Twenty yards away a figure had come out from the shadow of my neighbour's house, and was standing with his hands in his pockets looking up at the stars. Something in the way he stood suggested that it was Mr Gatsby himself.

I decided to call to him. Miss Baker had mentioned him at dinner, and that would do for an introduction. But I didn't call to him, for suddenly he did something which showed he was glad to be alone – he stretched out his arms towards the dark water, and, as far as I was from him, I could have sworn he was trembling. I looked towards the sea myself, and could see nothing except a single green light, very small and far away, on the coast of East Egg. When I looked once more for Gatsby he had gone, and I was alone again in the darkness.

Chapter 2   Mrs Wilson

About halfway between West Egg and New York, the motor road joins the railroad and runs beside it a short way to avoid an area of low ground which is being filled in with ashes. This grey land is always covered in clouds of dust, in which ash-grey men are working with spades on the piles of ash.

Above the dust you see an enormous pair of eyes, painted on a big board beside the road. Below the eyes is the name Doctor T. J. Eckleburg. The eyes of Dr T. J. Eckleburg look out of no face but, instead, from a pair of large, yellow glasses. I supposed that Dr Eckleburg had moved away from this unpromising area, leaving his advertisement behind him.

The train stops here, and it was because of this that I first met Tom Buchanan's lover.

The fact that he had one was mentioned by everyone who knew him. His friends did not approve of the way he brought her with him to popular cafés, as if to show her off to the world. Though I was interested to see her, I had no desire to meet her – but I did. I went up to New York with Tom on the train one Sunday afternoon, and when we stopped by the ash piles he jumped to his feet.

'We're getting off,' he insisted. 'I want you to meet my girl.' He took hold of my arm and forced me from the train.

We walked back along the road, under the fixed stare of Doctor Eckleburg. The only building in sight was a small block of yellow brick sitting on the edge of the wasteland. One of the three shops it contained was empty; another was an all-night café, with lines of ashes leading to the door. The third was a garage – *Repairs*. GEORGE B. WILSON. *Cars bought and sold*.

I followed Tom into the garage. The inside was empty and dirty, and the only car to be seen was the dust-covered wreck of an old Ford. The owner appeared in the door of an office. He was a pale, miserable man, who could have been good-looking if he were not so spiritless.

'Hello, Wilson, old man,' said Tom. 'How's business?'

'Not too bad,' said Wilson unhappily. 'When are you going to sell me that car?'

'Next week; I've got my man working on it now.'

Tom was looking impatiently around the garage, and in a moment the thickish figure of a woman appeared at the office door. She was in her mid-thirties, and there was no beauty in her face or body, but a kind of animal life force which made her strangely attractive.

She smiled slowly and, ignoring her husband as if he were not there, shook hands with Tom.

'Get some chairs, so somebody can sit down,' she said to her husband, who hurried into the office.

'I want to see you,' said Tom. 'Get on the next train.'

'All right.'

'I'll meet you by the newspaper shop.'

She moved away from him just as George Wilson came out of the office with two chairs.

We waited for her down the road and out of sight.

'Terrible place, isn't it?' said Tom. 'It does her good to get away. I rent an apartment in town for her, where I meet her sometimes.'

'Doesn't her husband mind?'

'Wilson? He thinks she goes to see her sister in New York. He's so stupid he'll believe anything.'

So Tom Buchanan, his girl and I went up together to New York – not quite together, for Mrs Wilson sat in another part of the train.

At the newspaper shop she bought a film magazine, and in the station drugstore some face cream. Outside the station we got into a taxi and drove off.

But immediately she stopped the taxi.

'I want to get one of those dogs,' she said. 'I want to get one for the apartment. They're nice to have – a dog.'

We stopped beside an old man with a basket full of very young dogs which he was selling.

'What kind are they?' asked Mrs Wilson.

'All kinds. What kind do you want, lady?'

'I'd like to get one of those police dogs; I don't suppose you got that kind?'

The man looked doubtfully into the basket and pulled up one of the animals by the back of the neck.

'That's no police dog,' said Tom.

'No, it's not exactly a police dog,' said the man.

'I think it's sweet,' said Mrs Wilson. 'How much is it?'

'That dog?' He looked at it admiringly. 'That dog will cost you ten dollars.'

'Is it a boy or a girl?' she asked delicately.

'That dog? That dog's a boy.'

'It's a female,' said Tom firmly. 'Here's your money. Go and buy ten more dogs with it.'

The dog changed hands and settled down on Mrs Wilson's knee. We drove over to Fifth Avenue, where I wanted to get out, but they both insisted that I go with them.

'I'll call up my sister Catherine,' said Mrs Wilson, 'and Mr and Mrs McKee from the apartment below.'

The apartment was on 158th Street. We went up to the top floor, and Mrs Wilson proudly opened the door. The small living room was filled with highly decorated furniture that was much too large for it.

Mrs Wilson sent a boy out to get some milk and dog food and a box for the dog, while Tom brought out a bottle of whisky from a locked cupboard.

Sitting on Tom's knee, Mrs Wilson telephoned her sister and the McKees, and invited them up. Then there were no cigarettes,

13

and I went out to buy some at the drugstore on the corner. When I came back they had both disappeared, so I sat down in the living room and waited. They came out of the bedroom just before the guests began to arrive.

I have been drunk just twice in my life, and the second time was that evening. So I don't have too clear a memory of most of the conversation. I remember that Mrs McKee had a loud, unpleasant voice, and her husband didn't say much.

The sister Catherine was an attractive girl of about thirty, who seemed to know rather more of the world than Mrs Wilson. She sat down beside me on the sofa.

'Do you live down on Long Island like Tom?' she inquired.

'I live at West Egg.'

'Really? I was down there at a party about a month ago. It was given by a man named Gatsby. Do you know him?'

'I live next door to him.'

'Well, they say he's a relative of King Wilhelm of Germany. That's where all his money comes from.'

'Really?' I didn't find this easy to believe.

Catherine was looking at Tom and Mrs Wilson. 'Myrtle and Tom look good together, don't they?' She leaned close to me and whispered in my ear: 'You know, they both *hate* the people they're married to. They ought to get a divorce and marry each other!'

I didn't answer, but she went on: 'It's really his wife that's keeping them apart. She's a Catholic, and they don't believe in divorce.'

Daisy was not a Catholic, and I was a little shocked at Tom's lie.

As the evening went on, the bottle of whisky – a second one – was in frequent demand by everybody except Catherine, who 'felt just as good on nothing at all'. Tom sent out for some sandwiches, which were a complete supper in themselves. I wanted to get out and walk towards the park as darkness fell, but each time I tried to go I became caught up in some wild, loud

14

argument. Then Myrtle pulled her chair close to mine, and suddenly poured over me the story of her first meeting with Tom.

'I was on the train going up to New York to see my sister, and he was sitting facing me. He had on a nice suit and a white shirt, and I couldn't keep my eyes off him, but every time I looked at him I had to pretend to be looking at the advertisement over his head. When we came into the station, he was next to me and his body was pressing against me. So I told him I'd have to call a policeman, but he knew I didn't mean it. When I got into a taxi with him I was so excited, I kept thinking, over and over, "You can't live for ever, you can't live for ever".'

It was nine o'clock – almost immediately afterwards I looked at my watch and found it was ten. The little dog was sitting on the table looking blindly through the smoke. Tom and Mrs Wilson stood face to face discussing whether Mrs Wilson had any right to mention Daisy's name.

'Daisy! Daisy! Daisy!' shouted Mrs Wilson. 'I'll say it whenever I want to! Daisy! Dai–!'

Making a short, sharp movement, Tom broke her nose with his open hand.

There was blood and confusion everywhere. While Catherine and Mrs McKee were comforting Myrtle and shouting at Tom, Mr McKee and I slipped out of the room and away.

Chapter 3   Meeting Mr Gatsby

There was music from my neighbour's house through the summer nights. In his blue gardens men and girls came and went, floating among the whisperings and the champagne and the stars. In the afternoon, by the shore, I watched his guests swimming in the Sound, or lying in the sun on the hot sand, or riding in his two motorboats.

At weekends his big, open car became a bus, carrying groups of people to and from the city between nine in the morning and long past midnight, while his second car met all the trains at the station. And on Mondays, eight servants, including the gardener, worked all day to repair the damage from the night before. Every Friday, five boxes of fruit arrived from a shop in New York – every Monday, the same fruit left his back door in a pile of empty halves.

About once in two weeks there was a really big party. The trees were all covered in coloured lights and a dance floor was laid down on the lawn; a big group of musicians came down from New York to play music for dancing. Wonderful food arrived, with lots of waiters to serve it, and in the main hall a bar was set up, serving every possible kind of alcoholic drink. I remember the sense of excitement at the beginning of the party.

By seven o'clock the last swimmers have come in from the beach and are dressing upstairs; cars from New York are arriving every minute, and already the halls and sitting rooms are full of girls in bright dresses with the newest, strangest hairstyles. Waiters are floating through the garden outside with an endless supply of drinks, until the air is alive with talk and laughter.

The lights grow brighter as darkness falls, and now the musicians are playing dance music and the voices are higher and louder. Laughter is easier minute by minute. The party has begun.

♦

I believe that on the first night I went to Gatsby's house I was one of the few guests who had actually received an invitation. People were not invited – they went there. They got into cars which carried them out to Long Island, and somehow they ended up at Gatsby's door. Once they were there, they were introduced to Gatsby by someone who knew him. Sometimes they came and went without having met Gatsby at all.

I had been actually invited. A driver in a pale blue uniform crossed my lawn early that Saturday morning with a surprisingly formal note from his employer: the honour would be Gatsby's, it said, if I would attend his 'little party' that night. He had seen me several times, and had intended to call on me, but something had always prevented it – signed Jay Gatsby.

I went over to his lawn a little after seven, and wandered around, feeling rather anxious among all these people I didn't know. As soon as I arrived I tried to find my host by asking various guests where he was. But they stared at me in such a surprised way that I gave up and made my way to the drinks' table – the only place in the garden where a single man could stand around without looking out of place.

I was still there some time later, when Jordan Baker came out of the house and stood at the top of the steps looking down into the garden.

'Hello!' I shouted, moving towards her.

'I thought you might be here,' she answered, as I came up. 'I remembered you lived next door to–'

She was interrupted by two girls in yellow dresses, who stopped at the foot of the steps.

'Hello!' they cried together. 'Sorry you didn't win.'

That was for the golf competition. She had lost in the last match the week before.

'You don't know who we are,' said one of the girls in yellow, 'but we met you here about a month ago.'

17

'You've changed the colour of your hair since then,' remarked Jordan.

With Jordan's golden arm resting on mine, we went down the steps and wandered around the garden. A waiter floated towards us, and we sat down at a table with the two girls in yellow and three men.

'I like to come to these parties,' said one of the girls. 'I never care what I do, so I always have a good time. When I was here last I tore my dress on a chair, and he asked me my name and address – a week later I got a package with a beautiful new evening dress in it. Two hundred and sixty-five dollars.'

'Did you keep it?' asked Jordan.

'Sure I did. I was going to wear it tonight, but it was too big around the top, and had to be made smaller.'

'There's something funny about a man that'll do a thing like that,' said the other girl. 'He doesn't want any trouble with anybody.'

'Who doesn't?' I inquired.

'Gatsby. Somebody told me . . .'

The two girls and Jordan leaned together.

'Somebody told me they thought he killed a man once.'

A current of excitement passed through all of us.

'I heard,' said one of the men, 'that he worked for the Germans during the war.'

'Oh no,' said the girl, 'he was in the American army.'

It seemed that Gatsby was a man everybody whispered about.

Supper was now being served, and Jordan invited me to join her group of friends, who were spread around a table on the other side of the garden. They were quiet, respectable people from East Egg, who seemed not to want to mix with the rest of the guests.

After half an hour Jordan whispered to me, 'Let's get out. This is much too polite for me.'

We got up, and she explained that we were going to find the host: I had never met him, she said, and that was obviously making me anxious.

The bar, where we looked first, was crowded, but Gatsby was not there. She couldn't find him from the top of the steps, and he wasn't on the porch. Then we tried an important-looking door, and walked into a great library.

A fat, middle-aged man with large, round glasses was sitting on the edge of a great table, staring unsteadily at the shelves of books. He looked drunk. As we entered, he turned and looked at us excitedly.

'What do you think?' he demanded.

'About what?'

He waved his hands towards the bookshelves.

'About the books. I thought they were just for show – but they're *real*! They have pages and everything. Look! Let me show you.' He pulled down a heavy, serious-looking book and opened it.

'Who brought you?' he demanded. 'I was brought by a woman I met somewhere last night. I've been drunk for about a week now, and I thought it might make me better to sit in a library.'

'Has it?'

'I can't tell yet. I've only been here an hour. Did I tell you about the books? They're real. They're–'

'You told us.' We went back outside.

There was dancing now in the garden, and the pairs of dancers moved in circles round the dance floor. A famous singer sang a song, some actors acted a funny scene, and champagne was served in glasses bigger than finger bowls. By midnight the fun was louder and wilder. From all over the garden happy, empty bursts of laughter rose towards the summer sky.

I was still with Jordan Baker. We were sitting at a table with a man of about my age and a girl who laughed all the time. I was enjoying myself now. I had taken two glasses of champagne, and the scene had changed before my eyes into something deep and meaningful.

The man looked at me and smiled.

'Your face is familiar,' he said politely. 'Weren't you in the army during the war? Perhaps we were in the same unit – were you in the First Division?'

'Why, yes.'

We talked for a moment about some wet, grey little villages in France. Obviously he lived in this neighbourhood, for he told me that he had just bought a seaplane, and was going to try it out in the morning.

'Want to go with me, old sport? Just near the shore along the Sound.'

I accepted. I was just going to ask his name when Jordan looked around and smiled. 'Having a good time now?'

'Much better.' I turned again to my new friend. 'This is an unusual party for me. I haven't even seen the host. I live over there–' I waved a hand in the direction of my house, 'and this man Gatsby sent over his driver with an invitation.'

For a moment he looked at me as if he didn't understand.

'I'm Gatsby,' he said suddenly.

'What!' I cried. 'Oh, I'm so sorry.'

'I thought you knew, old sport. I'm afraid I'm not a very good host.'

He smiled understandingly. It was one of those rare smiles with a quality of comfort in it, that you may come across four or five times in life. It seemed to face the whole world for a moment, and then fixed on *you*. It understood you as you wanted to be understood, and believed in you as you would like to believe in yourself. Then the smile disappeared, and I was looking at a fashionably dressed young man, a year or two over thirty, whose formal way of speaking was very nearly funny. Some time before he introduced himself I'd got a strong feeling that he was picking his words with care.

At this moment a butler hurried towards him with the information that Chicago was calling him on the telephone.

'Excuse me. I will rejoin you later,' he said politely.

When he was gone I turned to Jordan, to tell her of my surprise. I had expected Gatsby to be quite different – older, fatter, red-faced.

'Who is he?' I demanded. 'Do you know?'

'He's just a man named Gatsby.'

'Where is he from, I mean? And what does he do?'

'Now *you're* started on the subject,' she said with a pale smile. 'Well, he told me once he had been to Oxford University. But I don't believe it.'

'Why not?'

'I don't know. I just don't think he went there.'

There was really something very mysterious about Gatsby's background. Surely young men didn't just appear out of nowhere and buy a grand house on Long Island Sound?

The band began to play some loud music. At this moment my eye fell on Gatsby, standing alone on the steps and looking from one group to another with approving eyes. His skin was smooth and browned by the sun, and his short hair looked as if it was cut every day. I could see nothing mysterious about him. I wondered if the fact that he was not drinking helped to set him apart from his guests, for it seemed that he grew more correct as everyone else grew wilder. People were singing loudly, girls were falling backwards playfully into men's arms, but no one fell backwards on Gatsby.

Gatsby's butler was suddenly standing beside us.

'Miss Baker?' he inquired. 'Excuse me, but Mr Gatsby would like to speak to you alone.'

Jordan gave me a look of extreme surprise and followed the butler towards the house. I noticed that she wore her evening dress, all her dresses, like sports clothes.

An hour later I decided that it was time to go home. As I waited for my hat in the hall, the door of the library opened and Jordan and Gatsby came out together. He was speaking eagerly to her, until some other guests came up to say goodbye.

Jordan's friends were calling to her from the porch, but she came over to me. 'I've just heard the strangest thing,' she whispered. 'How long were we in there?'

'Why, about an hour.'

'It was so strange. But I promised I wouldn't tell it. Please come and see me . . . telephone book . . . under the name of Mrs Sigourney Howard . . . my aunt . . .' She was hurrying off as she talked.

The last of Gatsby's guests were standing around him. I felt rather guilty that on my first appearance I had stayed so late, and tried to explain that I'd hunted for him early in the evening.

'Don't mention it,' he said eagerly. 'And don't forget we're going up in the seaplane tomorrow morning, at nine.'

Then the butler, behind his shoulder: 'Philadelphia wants you on the phone, sir.'

'All right, I'll be there in a minute . . . Good night, old sport . . . Good night.' He smiled, and suddenly it seemed right to be among the last to leave, as if he had wanted it all the time.

♦

Reading over what I have written so far, I see I have given the idea that the events of three evenings were all that interested me. But in fact, at the time they were just some events among others in a crowded summer – they did not seem specially important to me until much later.

Most of the time I worked. My days usually followed the same

22

pattern: I arrived at my place of work in the early morning, and stayed there until the evening. I was friendly with the other clerks and lunched with them in dark, crowded restaurants. I took dinner usually at the Yale Club, and then I went to the library and studied money matters for an hour. After that I walked down Madison Avenue and over 33rd Street to the station, to catch my train back to West Egg.

For a while I lost sight of Jordan Baker, and then in midsummer I found her again. At first I was proud to go places with her, because she was a famous golf player and everyone knew her name. Then it was something more. I wasn't in love, but I felt a sort of gentle wish to understand her. The cold, scornful face that she turned to the world hid something – and one day I found what it was.

When we were at a house party together up in Warwick, she left a borrowed car out in the rain with the top down, and then lied about it. Suddenly I remembered the story about her that I'd tried to think of that night at Daisy's. At her first big golf match there was a scandal that nearly reached the newspapers – a suggestion that she had moved her ball in order to win.

Jordan Baker was dishonest. She couldn't bear to be at a disadvantage, so she used deceit to get what she wanted. In this way she was able to keep that cool, proud smile turned to the world. I realized that she avoided clever men. She felt safer with people who would not doubt her standards of behaviour.

It made no difference to me. Dishonesty in a woman is a thing you learn to accept – I was sorry, and then I forgot. It was at that same house party that we had a strange conversation about driving a car. It started because she drove too close to some workmen on the road.

'You ought to drive more carefully,' I told her.
'I am careful.'
'No, you're not.'

'Well, other people are. They'll keep out of my way.'

'Suppose you met somebody just as careless as yourself.'

'I hope I never will,' she answered. 'I hate careless people. That's why I like you.'

Her grey eyes stared straight ahead, but she had made a change in our relationship, and for a moment I thought I loved her. But I am full of rules that stop me from doing what I want to do. I knew that before I was free I had to break off that understanding with the girl back home, the girl I had been writing letters to once a week.

You see, I am one of the few honest people that I have ever known.

Chapter 4 Gatsby and Daisy

At nine o'clock one morning late in July, Gatsby's beautiful car pulled up outside my door. It was the first time he had visited me, though I had attended two of his parties, gone up in his seaplane and made frequent use of his beach.

'Good morning, old sport. You're having lunch with me today and I thought we'd drive up to town together.'

He saw me looking with admiration at his car.

'It's pretty, isn't it? Haven't you ever seen it before?'

I'd seen it. Everybody had seen it. It was enormous; a rich creamy yellow, with green leather seats. We set off.

I had talked with him a number of times in the past month and found, to my disappointment, that he had little to say. I had felt at first that he was someone who mattered, but now this feeling had disappeared: he had become simply the owner of a lovely house next door.

And then came that surprising ride. As we talked, Gatsby seemed strangely uncertain of himself, and began leaving his sentences unfinished. 'Look here, old sport,' he said suddenly, 'what's your opinion of me?'

I began making the kind of general remarks which that question deserves.

'Well, I'm going to tell you something about my life,' he interrupted. 'I don't want you to get a wrong idea of me from all these stories you hear. I'll tell you God's truth. I am the son of some wealthy people in the Middle West – all dead now. I was brought up in America, but educated at Oxford University, in England, because the men in my family were always educated at Oxford.'

He looked at me sideways – and I knew why Jordan Baker had believed he was lying. He hurried the phrase 'educated at Oxford', or swallowed it, as if it troubled him.

'My family all died and I was left a good deal of money. After that I lived like a lord in all the capitals of Europe – Paris, Venice, Rome – collecting jewels, hunting wild animals, painting a little, and trying to forget something very sad that happened to me long ago.'

With an effort I managed to hold back my laughter. I didn't believe a word of it.

'Then came the war, old sport. I was glad, and I tried very hard to die, but some magic seemed to keep me alive. I was made an officer when the war began, and put in charge of a machine-gun unit. In the Argonne Forest I took my men far in front of the foot soldiers. We stayed there for two days and two nights, 130 men with sixteen guns, and when the foot soldiers came up at last they found the flags of three German divisions among the piles of dead. I was given a higher rank, and every government on our side gave me a decoration – even Montenegro, little Montenegro down on the Adriatic Sea!'

He reached into his pocket, and pulled out a circle of metal on a coloured band.

'That's the one from Montenegro.'

To my surprise, the thing looked real. 'Captain Jay Gatsby,' I read, 'For Extraordinary Courage.'

'Here's another thing I always carry. A memory of Oxford days. It was taken in Trinity College.'

It was a photograph of six or seven young men standing in front of an old building, with towers behind them. There was Gatsby, looking a little, not much, younger.

Then it was all true. I imagined him in his palace in Venice, with tiger skins on the walls, staring into a chest of rich, dark jewels to take away the pain of his broken heart.

'I'm going to ask you to do a big thing for me today,' he said, 'so I thought you ought to know something about me. I didn't want you to think I was just some nobody.' He paused. 'You'll hear about it this afternoon.'

'At lunch?'

'No, this afternoon. I happened to find out that you're taking Miss Baker to tea.'

'Do you mean you're in love with Miss Baker?'

'No, old sport, I'm not. But Miss Baker has kindly agreed to speak to you about this matter.'

I hadn't the faintest idea what 'this matter' was, but I was more annoyed than interested. I hadn't asked Jordan to tea in order to discuss Mr Jay Gatsby.

He wouldn't say another word. We drove on, beside the valley of ashes. At Wilson's garage I caught sight of Mrs Wilson working the pump with her breathless animal energy.

Gatsby was driving very fast.

I heard the sound of a motorcycle, and a policeman rode up beside us. Gatsby stopped. Taking a white card from his pocket, he waved it before the man's eyes.

'Right you are!' agreed the policeman, raising his cap. 'Know you next time, Mr Gatsby. Excuse *me*!'

'What was that?' I inquired. 'The picture of Oxford?'

'I was able to do something for the Chief of Police once, and he sends me a Christmas card every year.'

◆

I met Gatsby for lunch in a little restaurant on 42nd Street. There was someone with him: a small, middle-aged man with a flat nose and small eyes.

'Mr Carraway, this is my friend Mr Wolfshiem.'

We sat down at our table and ordered our food.

'This is a nice restaurant,' said Mr Wolfshiem. 'But I like the old Metropole better, across the street.'

'It's too hot over there,' said Gatsby.

'Hot and small – but full of memories. Filled with faces dead and gone. I'll never forget the night they shot Rosy Rosenthal there. There were six of us at the table, and Rosy had been eating and drinking all evening. At four o'clock in the morning the waiter came up to him with a funny look and said somebody wanted to speak to him outside. I told him not to go.'

'Did he go?' I asked.

'Sure he went. He turned around in the door and said to us, "Don't let that waiter take away my coffee!" Then he went out into the street, and they shot him three times in his full stomach and drove away.'

He looked at me and said suddenly: 'I understand you're looking for a business connection.'

Gatsby answered for me. 'Oh, no, Meyer, this isn't the man! We'll talk about that some other time.'

We had nearly finished our meal when Gatsby looked at his watch, jumped up and hurried from the room.

'He has to telephone,' said Mr Wolfshiem. 'A business matter. Fine man, isn't he. A perfect gentleman. He went to Oxford College in England.'

'Have you known Gatsby for a long time?' I inquired.

'Some years. I met him just after the war, and we've done a lot of business – I've helped him and he's helped me.'

When Gatsby returned, Mr Wolfshiem took his leave.

'I'll leave you two young men to discuss your sports and your young ladies,' he said. We shook hands.

'Meyer Wolfshiem's quite a character around Broadway,' said Gatsby after he had gone.

'Who is he?' I asked. 'How did he make his money?'

'Oh, in various ways.' Gatsby paused. 'Do you remember that big sports scandal, back in 1919? Well, Meyer was responsible for that. He made a lot of money out of it.'

I was astonished. 'Why isn't he in prison?'

'They can't get him, old sport. He's a clever man.'

I insisted on paying the bill. As the waiter brought my change, I noticed Tom Buchanan across the crowded room.

'Come along with me for a minute,' I said to Gatsby. 'I've got to say hello to someone.'

When he saw us, Tom jumped up eagerly. 'Where've you been? Daisy's angry because you haven't telephoned.'

'This is Mr Gatsby, Mr Buchanan.'

They shook hands, and an unusual troubled look came over Gatsby's face.

'How've you been?' demanded Tom of me. 'How'd you happen to come up this far to eat?'

'I've been having lunch with Mr Gatsby.'

I turned towards Mr Gatsby, but he was no longer there.

♦

That afternoon, in the tea garden at the Plaza Hotel, Jordan Baker told me this story. The place was Louisville, the small midwest town where she grew up; the time was the year the United States entered the Great War.

One October day in 1917 – (said Jordan) – I was walking along the street where Daisy Fay lived. She was just eighteen, two years older than me, and by far the most popular of all the young girls in Louisville. I admired her a lot. She dressed in white, and had a little white car, and all day long the telephone rang in her house and excited young officers demanded to take her out that night.

When I came opposite her house that morning her car was in the road, and she was sitting in it with an officer I had never seen before. They were so interested in each other that she didn't see me until I was quite near.

'Hello, Jordan,' she called. 'Please come here.'

She asked if I was going to the Red Cross to sew things for

the soldiers. I was. Well then, she said, would I tell them that she couldn't come that day? While she was speaking, the officer looked at Daisy in a way that every young girl wants to be looked at sometimes. His name was Jay Gatsby, and I didn't lay eyes on him again for over four years – even after I'd met him on Long Island I didn't realize it was the same man.

That was 1917. By the next year I had a few young men myself, and I began to play in golf competitions, so I didn't see Daisy very often. She went with a slightly older crowd – when she went with anyone at all. There was a story going around that her mother had found her packing her bag one night to go to New York and say goodbye to a soldier who was going overseas. They stopped her, of course.

By the next autumn she was happy again, happy as ever, and in February she was said to be engaged to a man from New Orleans. In June she married Tom Buchanan of Chicago, with a ceremony like Louisville had never known before. He came down with a hundred people in four private cars, and hired a whole floor of the hotel, and the day before the wedding he gave her a string of jewels valued at three hundred and fifty thousand dollars.

I was an attendant at her wedding. The evening before, I came into her room half an hour before the grand dinner and found her lying on her bed as lovely as the June night in her flowered dress – and as drunk as a monkey. She had a bottle of wine in one hand and a letter in the other.

'Never had a drink before,' she said.

'What's the matter, Daisy?'

I was frightened: I'd never seen a girl in that state.

'Here, dearest.' She put her hand in a wastebasket and pulled out the string of jewels. 'Take them downstairs and give 'em back to whoever they belong to. Tell 'em all Daisy's changed her mind. Say: "Daisy's changed her mind!"'

She began to cry – she cried and cried. I rushed out and found her mother's servant, and we locked the door and got her into a cold bath. She wouldn't let go of the letter. She took it into the bath with her, until it was a wet ball.

But she didn't say any more. We put ice on her forehead and got her back into her dress, and half an hour later the jewels were around her neck and she went down to dinner.

Next day at five o'clock she married Tom Buchanan and started off on a three months' trip to the South Seas.

I saw them in Santa Barbara when they came back, and I thought I'd never seen a girl so crazy about her husband. If he left the room for a minute she'd say: 'Where's Tom gone?' and look worried until he came back again. She used to sit on the sand with his head on her knee, rubbing her fingers over his eyes and looking at him with deepest delight. That was August. A week after I left Santa Barbara, Tom had a car accident, which was reported in the newspapers. There was a girl with him, whose arm was broken – she was one of the girls working in the Santa Barbara hotel. That was the first of Tom's affairs.

The next April, Daisy had her child, and they went to France for a year or two. Then they came back to Chicago to settle down. They moved with a fast crowd, all of them young and rich and wild, but Daisy came out untouched by any scandal. Perhaps because she doesn't drink. It's a great advantage not to drink among hard-drinking people.

Well, about six weeks ago, she heard the name Gatsby for the first time in years. It was when I asked you – do you remember? – if you knew Gatsby in West Egg. After you had gone home she came into my room and woke me up, and said: 'What Gatsby?' and when I described him, she said in the strangest voice that it must be the man she used to know. It wasn't until then that I connected this Gatsby with the officer in her white car.

When Jordan had finished telling all this, we had left the Plaza and were driving through Central Park.

'It was a strange chance that brought him so near her,' I said.

'But it wasn't chance at all.'

'Why not?'

'Gatsby bought that house so that Daisy would be just across the bay.'

I remembered my first sight of Gatsby, staring out across the bay – it had not been the stars, then, which seemed to fill him with such feeling. Now he came alive to me.

'He wants to know,' said Jordan, 'if you'll invite Daisy to your house some afternoon and then let him come over.'

I was astonished that he should demand so little. He had waited five years and bought a great house – so that he could 'come over' some afternoon to a stranger's garden.

'Why didn't he ask you to arrange a meeting?'

'He wants her to see his house,' she explained. 'I think he half expected her to wander into one of his parties, but she never did. Then he began asking people if they knew her, and I was the first one he found.'

'Does Daisy want to see Gatsby?' I asked.

'She mustn't know. You just have to invite her to tea.'

It was dark now, and I put my arm around Jordan's golden shoulder and pulled her towards me and asked her to dinner.

Suddenly I wasn't thinking of Daisy and Gatsby any more. I tightened my arms around her. Her pale, scornful mouth smiled, and so I pulled her closer, this time to my face.

Chapter 5   The Tea Party

When I came home to West Egg at two in the morning, light was shining all over my garden. Turning a corner, I saw that it came from Gatsby's house, lit from top to bottom. At first I thought it was another party, but there wasn't a sound. As my taxi drove noisily away, I saw Gatsby walking towards me across his lawn.

'Your place looks like an entertainment hall,' I said.

He turned his eyes towards it. 'I have been looking into some of the rooms. Suppose we have a swim in the pool, old sport? I haven't used it all summer.'

'It's too late. I've got to go to bed.'

'All right.' He waited, looking at me eagerly.

'I talked with Miss Baker,' I said after a moment. 'I'm going to call up Daisy tomorrow and invite her over here to tea.'

'Oh, that's all right,' he said carelessly. 'I don't want to put you to any trouble.'

'What day would suit you?'

'What day would suit *you*?' he corrected me quickly.

'How about the day after tomorrow, at four o'clock?'

He thought for a moment. 'I want to get the grass cut.'

We both looked down at the grass – there was a sharp line where my untidy lawn ended and his well-kept one began. I suspected that he meant my grass.

'There's another little thing.' He paused. 'I thought – look here, old sport, you don't make much money, do you?'

'Not very much.'

'I thought you didn't, if you'll pardon my – you see, I carry on a little business on the side, a sort of sideline, you understand. And I thought that if you don't make very much – you're selling bonds, aren't you, old sport?'

'Trying to.'

'Well, this would interest you. It wouldn't take up much of your time and you might pick up a nice bit of money.'

In a different situation, that conversation might have changed my life. But I realized that his offer was made to repay me for the service I was about to perform for him – so how could I accept it?

'I've got my hands full,' I said. 'Thanks, but I couldn't take on any more work.'

I called up Daisy from the office next morning, and invited her to come to tea. 'Don't bring Tom,' I told her.

On the agreed day it was raining heavily. At eleven o'clock a man in a raincoat knocked at my door and said Mr Gatsby had sent him over to cut my grass. I remembered I had to go into the village to buy some cups and fresh fruit and flowers, and to ask my Finnish woman to come back.

The flowers were unnecessary, for at two o'clock a great pile of flowers arrived from Gatsby's, with a number of pots to hold them. An hour later there was a knock at the front door and Gatsby, in a white suit, silver shirt, and gold-coloured tie, hurried in. He was pale, and there were dark signs of sleeplessness beneath his eyes.

'Is everything all right?' he asked.

'The grass looks fine, if that's what you mean.'

'What grass?' he inquired. 'Oh, the grass out there.' He looked out of the window at it, but I don't believe he saw a thing. 'Have you got everything you need in the way of – tea?'

I took him into the kitchen. Together we examined the twelve cakes from the village shop.

'Will they do?' I asked.

'Of course, of course! They're fine!'

He sat down in the living room, and began turning the pages of one of my books. From time to time he looked miserably towards the window. Finally he got up and informed me, in an uncertain voice, that he was going home.

'Why's that?'

'Nobody's coming to tea. It's too late!'

'Don't be silly; it's just two minutes to four.'

At that moment there was the sound of a car turning into my drive. I went out into the yard and saw a large car coming up the drive. The driver stopped, and Daisy's face looked out at me with a delighted smile.

'Is this really where you live, my dearest one?'

Her musical voice was as exciting as ever. 'Are you in love with me,' she said low in my ear, 'or why did I have to come alone?'

'That's a secret. Tell your driver to go far away and spend an hour.'

We went in. To my great surprise, the living room was empty.

Then we heard a light knocking at the front door. I went and opened it. Gatsby, pale as death, was standing staring miserably into my eyes. He marched by me into the hall and disappeared into the living room.

For half a minute there wasn't a sound. I could feel my own heart beating loudly. Then I heard Daisy's clear voice.

'I certainly am very glad to see you again.'

I had nothing to do in the hall, so I went into the room.

Gatsby was leaning stiffly against the fireplace and Daisy was sitting on the edge of a hard chair. Neither of them was speaking.

'We've met before,' said Gatsby now, in a low voice.

'We haven't met for many years,' said Daisy flatly.

'Five years next November,' said Gatsby quickly, and there was another silence.

Then my Finnish woman brought in the tea, and we were able to keep ourselves busy by passing round cups and cakes. Daisy and I began to talk, and Gatsby looked from one to the other of us with unhappy eyes. After a little while I made an excuse and got to my feet.

'Where are you going?' demanded Gatsby anxiously.

'I'll be back.'

'I've got to speak to you about something before you go.' He followed me wildly into the kitchen, closed the door, and whispered 'Oh, God!' in a miserable way.

'What's the matter?'

'This is a terrible mistake,' he said, shaking his head from side to side. 'A terrible, terrible mistake.'

'You're just embarrassed, that's all,' and luckily I added: 'Daisy's embarrassed too.'

'She's embarrassed?' he repeated unbelievingly.

'Just as much as you are.'

'Don't talk so loud.'

'You're acting like a little boy,' I said impatiently. 'Not only that, but you're rude. Daisy's sitting in there all alone.'

He raised his hand to stop my painful words, gave me a worried look, and went back into the other room.

I walked out the back way, just as Gatsby had done earlier. It was raining hard again, and I ran to a large, black tree, whose thick leaves gave some shelter. There was nothing to look at from under the tree except Gatsby's enormous house, so I stared at it for half an hour.

Then the sun shone again, and I felt it was time to go back. I went in – after making every possible noise in the kitchen – but I don't believe they heard a sound. They were sitting at either end of the sofa, looking at each other, and all embarrassment was gone. Daisy's face was marked with tears, and when I came in she began drying her eyes in front of a mirror. But there was a change in Gatsby that was simply astonishing – his joy shone from him and filled the little room.

'Oh, hello old sport,' he said, as if he hadn't seen me for years.

'It's stopped raining.'

'Has it?' When he realized what I was talking about, he smiled happily and repeated the news to Daisy. 'What do you think of that? It's stopped raining.'

'I'm glad, Jay.'

'I want you and Daisy to come over to my house,' he said. 'I'd like to show her around.'

Daisy went upstairs to wash her face, while Gatsby and I waited on the lawn.

'My house looks good, doesn't it?' he demanded. 'See how the whole front of it catches the light.'

I agreed that it was lovely.

His eyes went over it, every curve, every straight line, every square tower.

'It took me just three years to earn the money that bought it.'

'I thought you were left your money by your father.'

'I was, old sport, but I lost most of it during the war.'

I think he hardly knew what he was saying, for when I asked him what business he was in he answered: 'That's my affair,' before he realized that it was a rude reply.

'Oh, I've been in several things,' he corrected himself. 'I was in the drugstore business and then I was in the oil business. But I'm not in either one now.'

Just then Daisy came out of the house.

'That enormous place *there*?' she cried, pointing.

'Do you like it?'

'I love it, but I don't see how you live there all alone.'

'I keep it always full of interesting people, night and day. People who do interesting things. Famous people.'

Instead of going across the lawn we went down the road and entered by the main gate. Daisy admired the view of the house standing dark against the sky, she admired the gardens, rich with sweet-smelling flowers.

It was strange to reach the wide steps and find no movement of bright dresses in and out of the door, and to hear no sound but bird voices in the trees. And inside, as we wandered through the great rooms, I felt that there were guests hidden behind every sofa and table, under orders to be silent until we had passed through.

We went upstairs, through old-style bedrooms full of fresh flowers, through dressing rooms and bathrooms with baths sunk in the floor. We went into one room where a young man was doing exercises on the floor. It was Mr Klipspringer, who was living in the house as Gatsby's guest. Finally we came to Gatsby's own rooms – a bedroom, a bathroom and a study – where we sat down and drank a glass of some Chartreuse he took from a cupboard in the wall.

He hadn't once stopped looking at Daisy, and I think he gave a new value to everything in his house according to how much she liked it. Sometimes, too, he stared around his possessions in a confused way, as though in her presence none of it was real any longer. Once he nearly fell down some stairs.

His bedroom was the simplest room of all – except that on the dressing table was a brush-and-comb set of pure, dull gold. Daisy took the brush with delight, and put it to her hair. Gatsby sat down and began to laugh.

'It's the funniest thing, old sport,' he said. 'I can't – when I try to –'

He had passed through two states and was entering a third. After his embarrassment and his joy he was now filled with wonder at her presence. He had been full of the idea of her for so long – it was a dream which he had dreamed right through to the end. Now the waiting was over.

He opened for us two great cupboards which held his suits and ties, and his shirts, in several high piles.

'I've got a man in England who buys me clothes. He sends over what he has chosen at the beginning of each season.'

He took out a pile of shirts and began throwing them, one by one, before us – shirts of fine cotton and thick silk, which covered the table in a confusion of many colours. While we admired them he brought more, and the soft, rich pile rose higher. Suddenly Daisy bent her head into the shirts and began to cry wildly.

'They're such beautiful shirts,' she cried. 'It makes me sad because I've never seen such – such beautiful shirts before.'

♦

After the house, we were going to see the gardens and the swimming pool, and the seaplane, and the midsummer flowers – but outside Gatsby's window it began to rain again, so we stood and looked at the misty surface of the Sound.

'If it wasn't for the mist we could see your home across the bay,' said Gatsby. 'You always have a green light that burns all night at the end of your sea wall.'

He seemed to be thinking. Perhaps he realized that the enormous importance of that light had now gone for ever. When he had been separated from Daisy by a great distance, the light had seemed very near to her, almost touching her. It had seemed as close as a star to the moon. Now it was just a green light on a wall.

I began to walk about the room, examining various objects. A large photograph of an oldish man in sailing clothes attracted me.

'Who's this?'

'That? That's Mr Dan Cody, old sport. He's dead now. He used to be my best friend years ago.'

'Come here *quick*!' cried Daisy at the window.

The rain was still falling, but in the west pink and gold clouds floated above the sea.

'Look at that,' she whispered. 'I'd like to get one of those pink clouds and put you in it and push you around.'

I tried to go then, but they wouldn't let me.

'I know what we'll do,' said Gatsby, 'we'll have Klipspringer play the piano.'

He went out of the room and came back with the young man, who looked embarrassed.

'I don't play well,' he said. 'I don't – hardly play at all. I'm out of practice –'

'We'll go downstairs,' interrupted Gatsby.

In the music room Gatsby turned on a single lamp beside the piano. He lit Daisy's cigarette with a shaking hand, and sat down with her on a sofa in a dark corner of the room.

When Klipspringer had played 'The Love Nest', he turned around unhappily.

'I'm all out of practice, you see, I told you I couldn't play. I'm all out of prac –'

'Don't talk so much, old sport,' ordered Gatsby. 'Play!'

Outside the wind was loud. All the lights were going on in West Egg now. It was time for me to go home.

As I went over to say goodbye, I saw an expression of uncertainty on Gatsby's face, as if he felt some doubt about his present happiness. Almost five years! All that time he had been building up his dream of her. How could any real person equal the enormous power of the dream? There must have been moments that afternoon when Daisy had disappointed him.

As I watched him, his expression changed. His hand took hold of hers, and when she whispered something in his ear he turned towards her with a rush of feeling. Her voice had a magic that was beyond all dreams.

They had forgotten me, but Daisy looked up and held out her hand; Gatsby didn't know me now at all. I went out of the room and down the wide steps into the rain, leaving them there together.

Chapter 6   Gatsby's Party

About this time a young reporter from a New York newspaper arrived one morning at Gatsby's door and asked him if he had anything to say.

'Anything to say about what?' inquired Gatsby politely.

'Why – any statement to give out.'

It appeared that he had heard people talking about Gatsby, and thought there should be a story there for the newspapers. Gatsby's fame was growing, but it was the wrong kind of fame. All summer the hundreds of people who had attended his parties were spreading stories about his past – stories that were completely untrue.

I had reached the point of believing everything and nothing about him. It was not until much later that I learnt the truth about his beginnings, when he told me himself. But I am going to bring it in at this point in my story, to clear away all the false ideas.

He wasn't Jay Gatsby at all at first. His name was James Gatz, and he lived in North Dakota. His parents were poor and unsuccessful farm people – in his imagination he had never really accepted them as his parents at all. In his own mind he was a completely different person. Every night as he lay in bed he was troubled by strange thoughts, dreams of an extraordinary and beautiful world which was quite beyond his experience. But someone like James Gatz did not belong in such a world: he needed to be a new person, to have a new name.

At the age of seventeen he invented Jay Gatsby, the kind of person he wanted to be. And to this idea of himself he was true until the end.

His new life began at the moment when he saw Dan Cody's boat on Lake Superior. For over a year James Gatz had been working his way along the south shore of Lake Superior, catching

41

fish or digging in the sand for shellfish, or doing anything that would bring him food and a bed. He was still searching for something to do on the day that Dan Cody's boat sailed into Little Girl Bay. It was a beautiful boat.

As he was wandering along the shore, he looked up and saw it stop in a dangerous area a little way from the shore. So he borrowed a rowboat, rowed out to the sailing boat, and informed its owner that a wind might catch it and break it up in half an hour.

I suppose he smiled at Cody – he had probably discovered that people liked him when he smiled. And when Cody asked him his name, he had the answer ready: Jay Gatsby.

Cody was fifty years old then, and a very rich man, from his gold and silver mines. He was still strong in body, but not in mind; and suspecting this, a number of women had chased him for his money, including Ella Kaye, the newspaper woman. He had been living on his boat, the *Tuomalee*, for five years, sailing along friendly shores, when he turned up in front of James Gatz.

To young Gatz, as he rowed out to the sailing boat, it represented all the beauty and wealth in the world.

When Cody asked him a few questions, he found that the boy was quick and determined to be successful, so he decided to employ him. A few days later he bought him a blue coat, six pairs of white trousers and a sailing cap. And when the *Tuomalee* left for the West Indies and the North African coast, Gatsby left too. He helped to sail the boat, acted as Cody's secretary, and sometimes even as his keeper. For when Dan Cody was drunk he was not responsible for his actions, and then he trusted in Gatsby to look after him. The arrangement lasted five years, during which the boat went three times around America. Then one night in Boston Ella Kaye came on board, and a week later Dan Cody died.

I remembered the photograph of him up in Gatsby's bedroom, a grey-looking man with a hard, empty face. He had been much too fond of women and drink – especially drink. That was the reason Gatsby drank so little himself. Sometimes during his parties women used to rub champagne into his hair; but apart from that, he formed the habit of keeping away from alcohol.

And it was Cody who left him money – twenty-five thousand dollars. But Gatsby never got the money: somehow, with the help of a clever lawyer, Ella Kaye managed to take all that remained of Cody's millions.

♦

For several weeks after my tea party for Daisy I didn't see Gatsby. Mostly I was in New York, going around with Jordan and trying to make myself pleasant to her old aunt. But finally I went over to Gatsby's house one Sunday afternoon. I'd been there only two minutes when somebody brought Tom Buchanan in for a drink. I was surprised, of course, but the really surprising thing was that it hadn't happened before.

There were three of them, riding horses – Tom and a man named Sloane and a pretty woman who had been there before.

'I'm delighted to see you,' said Gatsby, standing on his porch. 'I'm delighted that you dropped in. Sit right down. Have a cigarette.' He walked around the room quickly, ringing bells. 'I'll have something to drink for you in just a minute.'

Mr Sloane wanted nothing. A soft drink? No thanks. A little champagne? Nothing at all, thanks . . .

Gatsby turned to Tom.

'I believe we've met somewhere before, Mr Buchanan.'

'Oh, yes,' said Tom, polite, but obviously not remembering.

'About two weeks ago.'

'Oh, that's right. You were with Nick.'

'I know your wife,' continued Gatsby, almost angrily.

'Is that so?' Tom turned to me. 'You live near here, Nick?'

'Next door.'

'That so?'

Mr Sloane didn't enter into the conversation and the woman said nothing either – until suddenly, after two drinks, she became very friendly.

'We'll all come over to your next party, Mr Gatsby,' she suggested. 'What do you say?'

'Certainly; I'd be delighted to have you.'

'That would be very nice,' said Mr Sloane coldly. 'Well – think we ought to be going home.' He got to his feet.

'Why don't you stay for supper?' said Gatsby, who wanted to see more of Tom.

'You come to supper with me,' said the lady.

'Come along,' said Mr Sloane – to her only.

Gatsby wanted to go with them, and didn't see that Mr Sloane didn't want him. 'I haven't got a horse,' he said. 'I'll have to follow you in my car. Excuse me for just a minute.'

The rest of us went out on the porch, and Mr Sloane and the lady walked down the steps towards their horses.

'Where the devil did he meet Daisy?' said Tom angrily to me. 'I don't like her running around by herself.'

'Come on, Tom,' Mr Sloane called. 'We're late. We've got to go.' And then to me: 'Tell him we couldn't wait.'

They all rode quickly down the drive. When Gatsby came out of the front door with his hat and coat, they had disappeared.

Tom was obviously worried at Daisy's going around alone, for on the following Saturday night he came with her to Gatsby's party. Perhaps his presence there gave the evening its strange heaviness – it stands out in my memory from Gatsby's other parties that summer. There were the same people, the same enormous quantities of champagne, the same noise and many-coloured activity, but I felt an unpleasantness in the air that hadn't been there before.

Tom and Daisy arrived as it was getting dark, and we walked over the lawn among the bright crowds.

'These things excite me so,' Daisy whispered to me. 'If you want to kiss me at any time during the evening, Nick, just let me know and I'll be glad to arrange it for you.'

'Look around,' suggested Gatsby.

'I'm looking around. I'm having a wonderful—'

'You must see the faces of many people you've heard about.'

Tom's scornful eyes looked over the crowd. 'I was just thinking I don't know anyone here,' he said.

'Perhaps you know that lady.' Gatsby pointed to a fine creature, looking more like a beautiful flower than a woman, who sat under a tree surrounded by admirers. Tom and Daisy stared, recognizing a famous film star.

'She's lovely,' said Daisy.

'The man bending over her is her director.'

He took them formally from group to group:

'Mrs Buchanan . . . and Mr Buchanan – the polo player.'

'I've never met so many famous people,' Daisy said. 'I liked that man – what was his name? – with the sort of blue nose.'

Gatsby told her his name and added that he was a film producer.

'If you don't mind, I'd rather not be called the polo player,' said Tom pleasantly.

Daisy and Gatsby danced. I was surprised by his graceful, old-fashioned way of dancing. Then we wandered over to my house and they sat on the steps for half an hour, while I remained watchfully in the garden.

We returned to the party, and as we were sitting down to supper Tom appeared. 'Do you mind if I eat with some people over here?' he said.

'Go ahead,' answered Daisy, 'and if you want to take down any addresses, here's my little gold pencil.' She looked around after a moment and told me the girl with Tom was 'ordinary but pretty'. I knew then that except for the half-hour she'd been alone with Gatsby she wasn't having a good time.

The other people at our table were all rather drunk. Two weeks ago I had enjoyed these same people, but now their silly conversation annoyed me. It obviously offended Daisy. I could see that she disapproved of West Egg society.

I sat on the front steps with Daisy and Tom while they waited for their car.

'Who is this Gatsby?' demanded Tom suddenly. 'Some big bootlegger?'

'Where did you hear that?' I inquired.

'I didn't hear it. I guessed it. A lot of these newly rich people are just big bootleggers, you know.'

'Not Gatsby,' I said shortly.

'Well, he must have had to work hard to get this strange collection of people here tonight.'

'At least they are more interesting than the people we know,' said Daisy.

'You didn't look so interested.'

'Well, I was.' Daisy began to sing with the music, in her warm, magic voice. 'Lots of people come who haven't been invited,' she said suddenly. 'That girl hadn't been invited. They force their way in and he's too polite to send them away.'

'I'd like to know who he is and what he does,' insisted Tom. 'And I'm going to find out.'

'I can tell you right now,' she said. 'He owned some drugstores, a lot of drugstores. He built them up himself.'

Their car came up the drive at last.

'Good night, Nick,' said Daisy.

I stayed late that night. Gatsby asked me to wait until he was free, and I waited in the garden until the usual swimming party had run up, cold but happy, from the dark beach, until the lights went out in the guest rooms above. When he came down the steps at last, his eyes were tired.

'She didn't like it,' he said immediately.

'Of course she did.'

'She didn't like it,' he insisted. 'She didn't have a good time.'

He was silent, and obviously anxious.

'I feel far away from her,' he said. 'It's hard to make her understand.'

He told me then what he wanted. He wanted her to go to Tom and say: 'I never loved you.' Then, after she was free, they would go back to Louisville and be married from her house – just as if it was five years ago.

'And she doesn't understand,' he said. 'She used to be able to understand. We'd sit for hours–'

'You shouldn't ask too much of her,' I said. 'You can't repeat the past.'

'Can't repeat the past?' he cried unbelievingly. 'Why of course you can!'

He looked around him wildly, as if the past were hiding here in the shadow of his house, just out of reach of his hand.

'I'm going to fix everything just the way it was before,' he said firmly. 'She'll see.'

He talked a lot about the past, and I realized that he wanted to get something back, some idea of himself perhaps, that had gone into loving Daisy. His life had been confused and disordered since then, but if he could only return to a certain starting place and go over it all slowly, he could find out what that thing was . . .

One autumn night, he said, five years before, they had been walking down the street when the leaves were falling, and they came to a place where there were no trees and the street was white with moonlight. They stopped there and turned to each other.

His heart beat faster as Daisy's white face came up to his own.

47

He knew that when he kissed this girl he would lose some of his own power. He would for ever tie his dreams down to a human person – his grand imagination would no longer be free to wander through the universe. So he waited, listening for a moment longer to the music of the stars. Then he kissed her. At his lips' touch she became like a flower for him and the magic was complete.

Chapter 7   A Hot Afternoon

It was when interest in Gatsby was at its highest that the lights in Gatsby's house failed to go on one Saturday night. The cars which turned into his drive, expecting a party, stayed for a minute and then drove sadly away. Wondering if he were sick, I went over to find out.

The door was opened by an unfamiliar butler with an ugly face, who gave me a strange look.

'Is Mr Gatsby sick?'

'No.' After a pause he added, 'sir'.

'I hadn't seen him around, and I was rather worried. Tell him Mr Carraway came over.'

'Who?' he demanded rudely.

'Carraway.'

'Carraway. All right, I'll tell him.' He shut the door.

My Finnish woman informed me that Gatsby had dismissed every servant in his house a week ago, and replaced them with five or six others who never went into West Egg village but ordered supplies over the telephone. The general opinion in the village was that the new people weren't servants at all. Next day Gatsby called me on the phone.

'Going away?' I inquired.

'No, old sport.'

'I hear you dismissed all your servants.'

'I wanted somebody who wouldn't talk. Daisy comes over quite often – in the afternoons. These are people that Wolfshiem wanted to do something for. They're all brothers and sisters. They used to run a small hotel.'

'I see.'

He was calling up at Daisy's request – would I come to lunch at her house tomorrow? Miss Baker would be there. Half an hour later Daisy herself telephoned, and seemed glad to find that I was coming. Something was up.

The next day was boiling hot, the hottest day of the summer. Gatsby drove me over to the Buchanans' house.

The sitting room was well shaded against the sun, and it was dark and cool. Daisy and Jordan lay on the big sofa.

'We can't move,' they said together.

Jordan's fingers rested for a moment in mine.

'And Mr Thomas Buchanan, the polo player?' I inquired. Then I heard his voice in the hall, at the telephone.

Gatsby stood in the centre of the room and stared around. Daisy watched him and laughed her sweet, exciting laugh.

'That must be Tom's girl on the phone,' said Jordan.

We were silent. The voice in the hall rose high with annoyance: 'Very well, then, I won't sell you the car at all . . . and don't trouble me about it at lunchtime!'

'He's not really speaking into the telephone,' said Daisy.

'Yes, he is,' I said. 'It's a real deal. I happen to know about it.'

Tom threw open the door and hurried into the room.

'Mr Gatsby!' He put out his wide, flat hand with well-hidden dislike. 'I'm glad to see you, sir . . . Nick . . .'

'Make us a cold drink,' cried Daisy.

As he left the room again, she got up and went over to Gatsby and pulled his face towards her, kissing him on the mouth.

'You know I love you,' she whispered.

'You forget there's a lady present,' said Jordan.

At that moment a nurse came into the room, leading a little girl in a pretty white dress.

'My little sweetheart!' cried Daisy. 'Come to your mother!' The child rushed across the room to the sofa and hid her face in her mother's skirt.

'Oh, what a sweet thing! Stand up now and shake hands.'

Gatsby and I leaned down and took the small hand. Afterwards he kept looking at the child with surprise. I don't think he had ever really believed in its existence before.

'She doesn't look like her father,' said Daisy. 'She looks like me. She's got my hair and shape of the face.' She bent her face down to the child's neck. 'You little dream, you!'

Then she sat back on the sofa.

'Goodbye, my love!'

'Come, Pammy.' The nurse took the child's hand and pulled her out of the room.

Tom came back with our icy drinks. We drank thirstily.

'Come outside,' he suggested to Gatsby, 'I'd like you to have a look at the place.'

I went with them out to the porch. The Sound was green and still in the heat. Gatsby pointed across the bay.

'I'm right across from you.'

'So you are.'

We had lunch in the dining room, darkened too against the heat.

'What'll we do with ourselves this afternoon?' cried Daisy. 'And the day after that, and the next thirty years?'

'Don't worry,' said Jordan. 'Life starts all over again when it turns cool in the fall.'

'But it's so hot,' insisted Daisy, almost in tears, 'and everything's so confused. Let's all go to town!'

Tom was talking to Gatsby about his horses.

'Who wants to go to town?' demanded Daisy. Gatsby's eyes floated towards her. 'Ah,' she cried, 'you look so cool.'

Their eyes met, and they stared at each other, alone in space. With an effort she looked down at the table.

'You always look so cool,' she repeated. It was a way of saying that she loved him, and Tom Buchanan saw. He was astonished. His mouth opened a little, and he looked at Gatsby, and then back at Daisy.

'You look like the man in that advertisement,' she went on. 'You know the advertisement of the man–'

'All right,' interrupted Tom quickly, 'I'm perfectly happy to go to town. Come on – we're all going to town.'

He got up, his eyes still flashing between Gatsby and his wife. No one moved.

'Come on!' his temper was rising. 'What's the matter? If we're going to town, let's start.'

'Are we just going to go?' Daisy objected. 'Like this? Aren't we going to let anyone smoke a cigarette first?'

'Everybody smoked all through lunch.'

'Have it your own way,' she said. 'Come on, Jordan.'

They went upstairs to get ready while we three men went out onto the hot drive.

'Shall we take anything to drink?' called Daisy from an upper window.

'I'll get some whisky,' answered Tom. He went inside.

Gatsby turned to me.

'I can't say anything in his house, old sport.'

'She's got a voice which gives away her feelings,' I remarked. 'It's full of–' I paused.

'Her voice is full of money,' he said suddenly.

That was it. It was the voice of a rich girl – that was its magic. Tom came out of the house wrapping a bottle in a cloth, followed by Daisy and Jordan.

'Shall we all go in my car?' suggested Gatsby.

'No, you take mine,' said Tom, 'and let me drive yours.'

Gatsby did not like this idea.

'I don't think there's much gas,' he objected.

'If it runs out I can stop at a drugstore,' said Tom. 'You can buy anything at a drugstore these days.' He looked at Gatsby in a meaningful way.

A very strange expression passed over Gatsby's face.

'Come on, Daisy,' said Tom, pulling her towards Gatsby's car. He opened the door, but she moved away.

'You take Nick and Jordan,' she said. 'We'll follow in your car.'

She walked close to Gatsby, touching his coat. Jordan and Tom and I got into the front seat of Gatsby's car, and we drove off into the heat.

'Did you see that?' demanded Tom.

'See what?'

He looked at me sharply, realizing that Jordan and I must have known all the time about Daisy and Gatsby.

'I've found out some things about this man,' said Tom. 'I've made an inquiry into his past.'

'And you found he was an Oxford man,' said Jordan.

'An Oxford man! Never! He wears a pink suit.'

'Why did you invite him to lunch, then, if you feel like that about him?' demanded Jordan.

'Daisy invited him; she knew him before we were married – God knows where!'

We drove for a while in bad-tempered silence. Then as Doctor T. J. Eckleburg's eyes came into sight down the road, I remembered Gatsby's warning about the gas.

'We've got enough to get us to town,' said Tom.

'But there's a garage right here,' objected Jordan.

With an impatient sound Tom stopped the car under Wilson's sign. After a moment the owner came out from inside and stared miserably at the car.

'Let's have some gas!' cried Tom roughly. 'What do you think we stopped for – to admire the view?'

'I'm sick,' said Wilson, not moving. 'Been sick all day.'

'Well, shall I help myself?' Tom demanded. 'You sounded well enough on the phone.'

With an effort Wilson left the support of the doorway and began to work the pump. In the sun his face was green.

'I didn't mean to interrupt your lunch,' he said. 'But I need money pretty bad, and I was wondering what you were going to do with your old car.'

'How do you like this one?' asked Tom. 'I just bought it.'

'It's a nice yellow one,' said Wilson. 'But I could make some money on the other.'

'What do you want money for, all of a sudden?'

'I've been here too long. I want to get away. My wife and I want to go West.'

'Your wife does?' cried Tom.

'She's been talking about it for ten years. And now she's going whether she wants to or not. I just found out something funny is going on, and I'm going to get her away. That's why I've been asking you about the car.'

'What do I owe you?' demanded Tom sharply.

'One dollar twenty.'

I realized that so far he didn't suspect Tom. He had discovered that Myrtle had some sort of life apart from him in another world, and the shock had made him ill.

'I'll let you have that car,' said Tom. 'Tomorrow.'

Over the piles of ash, the enormous eyes of Doctor T.J. Eckleburg were watching, but when I turned round I realized that other eyes were also looking at us. In one of the windows over the garage the curtains had been pulled to one side, and Myrtle Wilson was staring down at the car. Her eyes, wide with jealous terror, were fixed not on Tom, but on Jordan Baker, whom she thought was his wife.

♦

Tom drove on towards New York at high speed. The confusion in his simple mind was obvious. An hour earlier he had been sure of his wife and his lover – and now they were both slipping rapidly out of his control. We caught up Gatsby and Daisy, and argued about how we were going to spend the hot afternoon. Jordan wanted to go to a cinema; Daisy suggested that we hire five bathrooms and take cold baths. In the end, for no very good reason, we decided to hire a sitting room in the Plaza Hotel. We all said it was a crazy idea but at least it was a place where we could drink something cool.

The room was large and airless, and opening the windows only let in some hot air from the Park. Daisy went to the mirror to fix her hair.

'Open another window!' she said, without turning round.

'There aren't any more windows.'

'Well, we'd better telephone for a hammer–'

'Forget about the heat,' said Tom impatiently. 'You make it ten times worse by complaining about it.'

'Why not let her alone, old sport?' remarked Gatsby.

There was a moment of silence.

'That's a great expression of yours,' said Tom sharply.

'What is?'

'All this "old sport" business. Where'd you get it from?'

'Now see here, Tom,' said Daisy, 'if you're going to make personal remarks I won't stay here a minute. Call up and order some ice for the drinks.'

Tom took up the telephone and gave the order. Then, for some reason, he and I started talking about our college days. Suddenly, Tom turned to Gatsby.

'By the way, Mr Gatsby, I hear you're an Oxford man.'

'Not exactly.'

'Oh, yes, I understand you went to Oxford.'

'Yes – I went there.'

A pause. Then Tom's voice, scornful and unbelieving: 'I wonder when that could have been.'

Another pause. A waiter came in with crushed ice, and closed the door softly. We all looked at Gatsby. This important detail was to be cleared up at last.

'I told you I went there,' he said.

'I heard you, but I'd like to know when.'

'It was in 1919. I only stayed five months – that's why I can't really call myself an Oxford man. It was an opportunity they gave to some of the officers after the war.'

I wanted to shout with joy. My belief in him returned.

Daisy smiled. 'Open the whisky, Tom. I'll pour you a drink.'

'Wait a minute. I want to ask Mr Gatsby one more question.'

'Go on,' Gatsby said politely.

'What kind of trouble are you trying to cause in my house?'

They were out in the open at last.

'He isn't causing trouble,' said Daisy. 'You're causing trouble, Tom. Please have a little control.'

'Control! I suppose these days you're expected to sit back and let Mr Nobody from Nowhere make love to your wife!'

'I've got something to tell you,' said Gatsby. 'Your wife doesn't love you. She's never loved you. She loves me.'

'You must be crazy!' cried Tom.

Gatsby jumped up. 'She only married you because I was poor and she was tired of waiting for me. It was a terrible mistake, but in her heart she never loved anyone but me!'

'Daisy!' said Tom. 'What's been going on?'

'I told you,' said Gatsby. 'Going on for five years.'

Tom turned to Daisy sharply.

'You've been seeing this person for five years?'

'Not seeing,' said Gatsby. 'No, we couldn't meet. But both of us loved each other all that time.'

'That's a lie!' Tom burst out. 'Daisy loved me when she married me and she loves me now. And I love Daisy too. Once in

56

a while I go off on a little adventure, but I always come back, and in my heart I love her all the time.'

'You're disgusting,' said Daisy. She turned to me. 'Do you know why we left Chicago? You didn't hear the story of that "little adventure"?'

'Daisy, that doesn't matter now,' said Gatsby. 'Just tell him the truth – that you never loved him.'

She looked at him blindly. 'Why – how could I love him?'

'You never loved him.'

She paused. 'I never loved him,' she said slowly.

'Not on our wedding trip?' demanded Tom. 'Not that day I carried you down the hill to keep your shoes dry?' There was a gentleness in his voice . . . 'Daisy?'

'Please don't.' Her hand was shaking as she tried to light a cigarette. Suddenly, she threw the cigarette and the burning match on the floor.

'Oh, you want too much!' she cried to Gatsby. 'I love you now – isn't that enough? I can't help what's past. I did love him once – but I loved you too.'

'Even that's a lie,' said Tom. 'She never thought of you.' The words seemed to bite into Gatsby.

'I want to speak to Daisy alone,' he said.

'Even alone I can't say I never loved Tom.' Her voice was shaking. 'It wouldn't be true.'

'Of course it wouldn't,' said Tom. 'And from now on I'm going to take care of you, Daisy.'

'You don't understand,' said Gatsby. 'You're not going to take care of her any more.'

'I'm not?' Tom opened his eyes wide and laughed. He could afford to control himself now. 'Why's that?'

'Daisy's leaving you.'

'Nonsense.'

'I am, though,' she said with an effort.

Tom ignored her. 'She's not leaving me! Certainly not for someone as dishonest as you! Who are you? You hang around with Meyer Wolfshiem – I've been looking into your affairs.'

'I won't stand this!' cried Daisy. 'Oh, let's get out!'

'I found out what your drugstores were.' He turned to us. 'He and this Wolfshiem bought up a lot of side-street drugstores here and in Chicago, and used them to sell alcohol. My friend Walter told me. But now they're concerned with something bigger – Walter's afraid to tell me about it.'

I looked at Gatsby, and the expression on his face frightened me. It passed, and he began to talk excitedly to Daisy. But with every word she was drawing further and further into herself, so he gave up. Whatever courage she had had was definitely gone. She begged again to go.

'Please Tom! I can't stand this any more.'

'You two go home, Daisy,' said Tom. 'In Mr Gatsby's car. Go on. He won't annoy you now – he realizes it's over.'

They went, without a word. After a moment Tom got up and began wrapping the unopened bottle of whisky in the cloth.

'Want any of this? Jordan? Nick?'

I didn't answer.

'Nick?'

'What?'

'Want any?'

'No . . . I just remembered that today's my birthday.'

I was thirty.

It was seven o'clock when we got into the car with him and set off for Long Island.

Thirty – the promise of loneliness in front of me. A thinning list of unmarried friends, thinning hair. But there was Jordan beside me, who was wiser than Daisy. As we drove, her pale face fell lazily against my shoulder.

So we drove on through the falling darkness towards death.

Chapter 8   Accident

The main witness to the accident was the young Greek, Michaelis, who ran the café beside the ash piles. He told his story later, at the inquiry.

Some time after five he had wandered over to the garage and found George Wilson sick in his office – really sick, pale as his own pale hair and shaking all over. Michaelis advised him to go to bed, but he refused. Then they heard a violent noise upstairs.

'I've got my wife locked in up there,' explained Wilson. 'She's going to stay there until the day after tomorrow, and then we're going to move away.'

Michaelis was astonished; they had been neighbours for four years, and Wilson did not seem the kind of man who had the strength to do such a thing. So naturally Michaelis tried to find out what had happened. But Wilson wouldn't say a word – instead he began to question his visitor as if he suspected him, asking him what he'd been doing at certain times on certain days. Michaelis went back to his café.

When he came out again around seven he heard Mrs Wilson's voice, loud and angry, in the garage. A moment later she rushed out into the road, waving her hands and shouting.

The 'death car', as the newspapers called it, didn't stop; it came out of the growing darkness, slowed down for a moment, and then disappeared around the next bend. The other car, the one going to New York, stopped a hundred yards further on, and its driver hurried back to where Myrtle Wilson lay in the road, her thick, dark blood mixing with the dust.

♦

We saw the cars and the crowds when we were still some distance from the garage. 'A crash!' said Tom. 'We'll take a look.' He stopped the car, and we got out. We saw the serious faces of the people at the garage door, and we could hear a strange groaning sound coming from inside.

'There's some bad trouble here,' said Tom excitedly.

He looked over a circle of heads into the garage. Then he made a rough sound in his throat and with a violent movement pushed his way through. Jordan and I followed when we were able to.

Myrtle Wilson's body lay on a work table by the wall, and Tom was bending over it. Next to him stood a policeman, taking down names in a little book. The groaning sound was coming from Wilson, who was standing in the doorway of his office, rocking backwards and forwards and making his high, terrible call: 'Oh, my God! Oh, my God! Oh, my God!'

Tom turned to the policeman.

'What happened? That's what I want to know.'

'Car hit her. Killed immediately. She ran out into the road. Driver didn't even stop his car.'

'It was a yellow car,' said a man. 'Big, yellow car.'

Wilson seemed to hear this. 'You don't have to tell me what kind of car it was. I know what kind of car it was!'

Tom walked over to Wilson and put his hands on his arms. 'Listen. I just got here, from New York. I was bringing you my car. That yellow car I was driving this afternoon wasn't mine – do you hear?' He picked up Wilson, carried him into the office and set him down in a chair.

'Let's get out,' he whispered to me, and we pushed our way through the crowd and out to the car.

As the car raced through the night, I heard a low sound and saw that the tears were flowing down Tom's face.

'He didn't even stop his car,' he said.

♦

Suddenly we were outside the Buchanans' house.

'Daisy's here,' said Tom, looking up at two lighted windows.

Then he turned to me. 'I ought to have dropped you in West Egg, Nick. I'll telephone for a taxi to take you home. You and Jordan can go into the kitchen and the servants will get you some supper – if you want any.'

'No, thanks. But I'd be glad if you'd order the taxi.'

Jordan put her hand on my arm. 'Won't you come in, Nick? It's only half past nine.'

'No, thanks.' I was feeling a little sick and I wanted to be alone. I'd had enough of all of them for one day, and suddenly that included Jordan too. She must have seen something of this in my expression, for she turned sharply away and ran up the steps. I began walking down the drive.

A moment later I heard my name, and Gatsby stepped from between two bushes.

'What are you doing?' I inquired.

'Just standing here, old sport.' After a minute he asked, 'Did you see any trouble on the road?'

'Yes.'

He paused. 'Was she killed?'

'Yes.'

'I thought so; I told Daisy I thought so. It's better that the shock should all come at once. She took it quite well.' He spoke as if the effect of the accident on Daisy was the only thing that mattered.

'I got to West Egg by a side road,' he went on, 'and left the car in my garage. I don't think anybody saw us.'

I felt so angry with him, I didn't tell him he was wrong.

'Who was the woman?' he inquired.

'Her name was Wilson. Her husband owns the garage. How ever did it happen?'

'Well, I tried to turn the wheel–' He stopped, and suddenly I guessed at the truth.

'Was Daisy driving?'

'Yes,' he said after a moment. 'But of course I'll say I was. You see, when we left New York she was very upset, and she thought it would help her to drive. This woman rushed out at us just as we were passing a car coming the other way. It seemed to me that she wanted to speak to us – that she thought we were somebody she knew. Well, first Daisy turned away from the woman towards the other car, then she was afraid and turned back. I felt the shock as we hit her. I tried to make Daisy stop, but she couldn't.

'She'll be all right tomorrow,' he went on. 'I'm just going to wait here in case Tom tries to hurt her.'

'He won't touch her. He's not thinking about *her*. How long are you going to wait?'

'All night, if necessary. Well, until they go to bed.'

I looked at the house; there were two or three lighted windows downstairs. 'You wait here,' I said. 'I'll see if there's any sign of trouble.'

I walked silently over the lawn to the kitchen window.

Daisy and Tom were sitting opposite each other at the kitchen table, with a plate of cold chicken between them, and two bottles of beer. Tom was talking, and from time to time Daisy moved her head in agreement. They weren't happy, and they hadn't touched the food and drink – and yet they weren't unhappy either. They looked as if they were planning something together.

As I went back to Gatsby, I heard my taxi arriving.

'It's all quiet up there. Come home and get some sleep.'

'No, I want to wait here until Daisy goes to bed. Good night, old sport.' He turned to look eagerly at the house.

So I walked away and left him standing there in the moonlight – watching over nothing.

Chapter 9   Murder

I hardly slept all night. Around four I heard a taxi go up Gatsby's drive, and immediately I jumped out of bed and began to dress. I felt I had something to tell him, something to warn him about, and morning would be too late.

Crossing his lawn, I saw that his front door was still open. He was in the hall, leaning heavily on a table.

'Nothing happened,' he said. 'I waited, and at last she came to the window and stood there for a minute and then turned out the light.'

He wanted a cigarette, and we began hunting through the great rooms for the cigarette box. That night his house seemed to me more enormous than ever – and strangely dusty, as if no one was living there. There were only two old cigarettes left in the box. We threw open the sitting-room windows and sat smoking out into the darkness.

'You ought to go away,' I said. 'They're sure to find your car.'

'Go away now, old sport?'

He wouldn't consider it. He couldn't possibly leave Daisy until he knew what she was going to do. He was hanging onto some last hope that she might leave Tom, and I couldn't bear to tell him there was no longer any hope.

It was this night that he told me the strange story of his youth with Dan Cody. He told me because 'Jay Gatsby' had broken up like glass against Tom's hardness, and didn't exist any more – the long game was over.

He wanted to talk about Daisy. She was the first 'nice' girl he had ever known. He found her excitingly desirable. He went to her house, at first with other officers from the army camp, then alone. It astonished him – he had never been in such a beautiful house before. And because Daisy lived there, it had a feeling of mystery about it.

But he knew that he was in Daisy's house by accident. She knew nothing about him. He had let her believe that he was from the same sort of background as herself – that he was fully able to take care of her. He didn't tell her that he had no comfortable family standing behind him. He might have a golden future as Jay Gatsby, but at present he was a penniless young man without a past. His soldier's uniform protected him, but when he lost that, he would be a nobody. So he made the most of his time. He took what he could get – and in the end he took Daisy, one quiet October night.

He had intended, probably, to take what he could and go – but now he found that he could not pull himself away from Daisy. He knew that Daisy was extraordinary, but he didn't realize just how extraordinary a 'nice' girl could be. She disappeared that night into her rich house, into her rich, full life, leaving Gatsby – nothing. He felt married to her, that was all.

♦

'I can't tell you how surprised I was to find out I loved her, old sport. I even hoped for a while that she would throw me over, but she didn't, because she was in love with me too. She thought I knew a lot because I knew different things from her. Well, there I was, going in quite the wrong direction to succeed in my plans for my life. I was getting deeper in love every minute, and all of a sudden I didn't care about my plans. What was the use of doing great things if I could have a better time telling her what I was going to do?'

On the last afternoon before he went abroad, he sat silently with Daisy in his arms for a long time. It was a cold fall day, with a fire in the room. Now and then she moved and he changed the position of his arm a little, and once he kissed her dark, shining hair. The afternoon had made them calm, as if to give them a deep memory for the long separation that was to come. They had never been closer in their month of love.

♦

He did surprisingly well in the war. He was made a captain even before he went to fight in France, and following the Argonne battles he was put in command of his unit. After the war was over he tried hard to get home, but for some reason he was sent to Oxford instead. He was worried now by Daisy's letters. She didn't see why he couldn't come. She wanted to see him and feel him beside her, to be sure that she was doing the right thing.

For Daisy was young, and she was feeling the pressure of the world around her, where her friends danced all night. She began to move again with the season; suddenly she was accepting lots of invitations from lots of different men. And all the time something inside her was crying for a decision. She wanted her life shaped now, immediately – and the decision must be made by some force that was close at hand.

That force took shape in the middle of spring with the arrival of Tom Buchanan. There was a solidness about his person and his position, and Daisy decided to put her future in his hands. The letter announcing her engagement reached Gatsby while he was still at Oxford.

♦

It was getting light now on Long Island and we went around opening the rest of the windows downstairs.

'I don't think she ever loved him.' Gatsby turned around from a window. 'She was very excited this afternoon – she hardly knew what she was saying.'

He sat down with a look of hopelessness.

'Of course, she might have loved him for just a minute, when they were first married – and loved me more even then, do you see?'

He had come back from France when Tom and Daisy were still on their wedding trip, and made a miserable journey to Louisville on the last of his army pay. He stayed there a week, walking the streets where they had walked together. When he left on the bus, he was penniless.

It was nine o'clock when we finished breakfast and went out on the porch. The night had made a sharp difference to the weather, and there was a touch of autumn in the air. The gardener, the last one of Gatsby's former servants, came to the foot of the steps.

'I'm going to empty the pool today, Mr Gatsby. Leaves'll start falling soon, and there'll be trouble with the pipes.'

'Don't do it today,' Gatsby said. He turned to me. 'You know, old sport, I've never used that pool all summer.'

I looked at my watch and stood up.

'Twelve minutes to my train.'

I didn't want to go to the city. I didn't feel like work, but it was more than that – I didn't want to leave Gatsby. I missed that train, and then another, before I could get myself away.

'I'll call you up,' I said finally. 'About twelve.'

'Do, old sport.'

We walked slowly down the steps.

'I suppose Daisy'll call too.' He looked at me anxiously.

'I suppose so.'

'Well, goodbye.'

We shook hands and I set off. Just before I reached my garden I remembered something and turned around.

'They're no good, any of them!' I shouted across the lawn, and

I meant Tom and Daisy, and all Gatsby's fashionable 'friends'. 'You're worth the whole lot of them!'

I've always been glad I said that. It was the only praise I ever gave him, because I disapproved of him from beginning to end. He raised his hand politely, then his face broke into that wonderful, understanding smile of his, as if the two of us were close together in a secret world.

'Goodbye,' I called. 'I enjoyed breakfast, Gatsby.'

♦

Up in the city, I tried for a while to write out a long list of figures, then I fell asleep in my chair. Around midday the phone woke me. It was Jordan Baker, who often called me up at this hour, because it was difficult for me to call her. Usually her voice came over the line as something fresh and cool, but today it seemed sharp and dry.

'I'm going down to Southampton this afternoon.' She paused. 'You weren't so nice to me last night.'

This made me angry. 'Last night, nothing mattered.'

Silence for a moment. Then: 'But – I want to see you.'

'I want to see you, too.'

'Suppose I don't go to Southampton, and meet you in town instead?'

'No, I don't think this afternoon.'

'Very well.'

'It's impossible this afternoon. Various–'

We talked like that for a while, and then suddenly we weren't talking any longer. I don't know which of us hung up, but I know I didn't care.

I called Gatsby's house a few minutes later, but the line was busy. I tried four times; finally the operator told me the line was being kept open for a call from Detroit. Taking out my timetable,

I drew a small circle around the 3.50 train. It was just twelve o'clock.

♦

Now I want to go back a little and tell what happened at the garage after we left. The story was told later at the inquiry by Michaelis, the owner of the café.

All night he had stayed with Wilson. Until long after midnight the garage was full of people. They left at last, and Michaelis was alone with Wilson, who was still rocking backwards and forwards and groaning. About three o'clock he grew quieter, and began to talk about his wife. He said that a few months ago she had come home from the city with her nose cut and bleeding.

'I thought then there was something funny going on. And yesterday afternoon I found this.' He opened a drawer in the desk and pulled out an expensive dog collar.

'I found this among her things. She tried to explain it, but I could see she was lying – I knew then she had some other man. I took her to the window,' – with an effort he got up and walked to the window and leaned with his face pressed against it – 'and I said, "God knows what you've been doing, everything you've been doing. You may deceive me, but you can't deceive God – God sees everything!"'

Standing behind Wilson, Michaelis saw with a shock that he was looking at the eyes of Doctor T. J. Eckleburg, pale and enormous in the early morning light.

'That's an advertisement!' Michaelis told him.

'And then he killed her,' said Wilson.

'Who did?'

'The man in the yellow car – her lover. She ran out to speak to him and he wouldn't stop. He *murdered* her. Well, I'm going to find out who that yellow car belongs to.'

♦

By six o'clock Wilson seemed quiet, and Michaelis went home to sleep. When he awoke four hours later and hurried back to the garage, Wilson was gone.

The police were later able to follow his movements as far as Gad's Hill. He was on foot all the time, and various people had seen a man on the road 'acting sort of crazy'. He reached Gad's Hill at about twelve o'clock, and bought a sandwich that he didn't eat. Then for two hours he disappeared from view. The police supposed that he spent that time going from garage to garage, inquiring for a yellow car. But no garage man who had seen him ever came forward. Perhaps he had an easier, surer way of finding out what he wanted to know. By half past two he was in West Egg, where he asked someone the way to Gatsby's house. So by that time he knew Gatsby's name.

◆

At two o'clock Gatsby put on his swimsuit and told the butler that if anyone phoned he should bring word to him at the pool. He went to the garage for a water bed that had amused his guests during the summer, and the driver helped him to pump it up. Then he gave orders that the open car wasn't to be taken out for any reason – and this was strange, because the front was damaged on the right side and needed repair.

Gatsby picked up the bed and started for the pool.

No telephone message arrived, from Daisy or anyone else. The butler went without his sleep and waited for it until four o'clock – until long after there was anyone to give it to. I have an idea that Gatsby himself didn't believe it would come, and perhaps he no longer cared.

The driver heard the shots – afterwards he only said that he hadn't thought anything much about them. No one went near the pool until I arrived from the station and rushed anxiously up the front steps. Then we hurried down to the pool, the driver, butler, gardener and I.

There were small waves on the water, and the water bed with its load was moving down the pool. We could a red line spreading from it through the water.

It was as we were carrying Gatsby's body towards the house that the gardener saw the body of Wilson a little way off in the grass. The destruction was complete.

Chapter 10   Saying Goodbye

Two years later I remember the rest of that day, and that night and the next day, only as an endless stream of police and photographers and newspapermen in and out of Gatsby's front door. I said as little as possible myself. One policeman used the word *crazy* as he bent over Wilson's body that afternoon; and the newspaper reports the next day took up this idea.

Later, at the inquiry, Michaelis's story showed that Wilson had suspected his wife of having an affair with another man. I thought then that the whole story might come out – but Myrtle's sister Catherine, who might have said so much, didn't say a word. She swore that her sister had never seen Gatsby, that her sister had been completely happy with her husband, that her sister had been in no trouble at all. So the decision reached by the inquiry was that Myrtle Wilson had been accidentally killed by a stranger; and George Wilson, driven crazy by grief, had followed the track of this stranger, shot him and then shot himself. The case was closed.

But all this part of it didn't seem to matter. What mattered was that I found myself on Gatsby's side, and alone. From the moment I telephoned news of the murder to West Egg village, every question and every inquiry about him was addressed to me. At first I was surprised and confused; then, as he lay in his house and didn't move or breathe or speak, hour after hour, it grew on me that I was responsible, because no one else was interested.

I called up Daisy half an hour after we found him. But she and Tom had gone away early that afternoon.

'Left no address?'

'No.'

'Any idea where they are? How could I reach them?'

'I don't know. Can't say.'

I wanted to get somebody for him. I wanted to go into the

71

room where he lay and promise him: 'I'll get somebody for you, Gatsby. Don't worry. Just trust me.'

I tried to telephone Meyer Wolfshiem, but he wasn't in. Then I went upstairs and looked quickly through the unlocked parts of his desk – he'd never told me definitely that his parents were dead. But there was nothing – only the picture of Dan Cody staring coldly down from the wall.

Next morning I sent the butler to New York with a letter to Wolfshiem, asking him to come out on the next train. I was sure he'd come, when he saw the newspapers, just as I was sure there'd be a message from Daisy. But neither arrived. The butler brought back a letter from Wolfshiem. 'This has been a terrible shock to me. But I cannot come down now as I am tied up in some very important business and cannot get mixed up in this thing.'

When the phone rang that afternoon and the operator said there was a call from Chicago, I thought this would be Daisy at last. But it was a man's voice on the phone.

'This is Slagle speaking . . .'

'Yes?' I didn't know the name.

'Young Parke's in trouble. The police got him when he tried to sell those stolen bonds – they'd just got a message from New York giving them the numbers—'

'Look here!' I interrupted. 'This isn't Mr Gatsby. Mr Gatsby's dead.'

There was a long silence, followed by a cry of fear, and the caller hung up suddenly.

♦

I think it was on the third day that a message signed Henry C. Gatz arrived from a town in Minnesota. It said only that the sender was coming immediately.

He came. It was Gatsby's father, a grave old man, in a tired, miserable state.

'I saw it in the Chicago newspaper,' he said. 'It was all in the newspaper. I started right away.'

'I didn't know how to reach you.'

His eyes moved about the room, seeing nothing.

'It was a crazy man,' he said. 'He must have been crazy.'

'Wouldn't you like some coffee?' I said.

'I don't want anything. Where have they got Jimmy?'

I took him into the room where his son lay, and left him there. After a little while he came out, his mouth open, and a few tears on his face. He had reached an age where death no longer has the quality of terrible surprise; and when he looked around him now and saw the height and beauty of the hall and the great rooms opening out from it, his grief began to be mixed with pride. I helped him to a bedroom upstairs, and told him that all arrangements for the funeral had been put off until he came.

'I didn't know what you'd want, Mr Gatsby–'

'Gatz is my name.'

'Mr Gatz. I thought you might want to take the body back West.'

He shook his head. 'Jimmy always liked it better down East. He rose up to his position here. Were you a friend of his?'

'We were close friends.'

'He had a big future before him, you know. If he'd lived, he would have been a great man. He'd have helped build up the country.'

'That's true,' I said, uncomfortably.

He lay down stiffly, and was immediately asleep.

That night I had a call from Klipspringer, the young man who had been Gatsby's house guest for so long. That would be another friend at Gatsby's grave.

'The funeral's tomorrow,' I said. 'Three o'clock, here at the house. I wish you'd tell anybody who'd be interested.' I didn't want to put it in the newspapers and draw a sightseeing crowd, so I'd been calling up people myself. They were hard to find. 'Of course, you'll be there yourself.'

'Well, I don't think I . . . What I called up about was a pair of shoes I left there. Could you ask the butler to send them on? You see, they're tennis shoes, and I'm sort of helpless without them. My address is—'

I didn't hear his address, because I hung up in disgust.

The morning of the funeral I went up to New York to see Meyer Wolfshiem. He drew me into his office, remarking that it was a sad time for all of us.

'My memory goes back to when I first met him,' he said. 'He was looking for a job. A young officer just out of the army and covered over with decorations he got in the war. He was so poor he had to keep on wearing his uniform because he couldn't buy some ordinary clothes. He hadn't eaten anything for a few days. "Come and have lunch with me," I said. He ate more than four dollars' worth of food in half an hour.'

'Did you start him in business?' I inquired.

'Start him! I made him. I raised him out of nothing. I saw he was a gentlemanly-looking young man, and when he told me he was at Oxford I knew I could use him. He did some work for a friend of mine right away. We were like that,' — he held up two fat fingers — 'always together.'

'Now he's dead,' I said after a moment. 'You were his closest friend, so you'll want to come to his funeral this afternoon.'

'I can't do it — I can't get mixed up in it,' he said. 'When a man gets killed, I never get mixed up in it.'

I went home to West Egg, changed my clothes and went next door. It was raining. I found Mr Gatz walking up and down excitedly in the hall. His pride in his son and in his son's possessions was continually increasing.

'Had you seen your son recently?' I asked.

'He came out to see me two years ago, and bought me the house I live in now. He was always very generous to me.'

A little before three the minister from the church arrived, and I began to look out of the windows for other cars. The servants came in and we all stood waiting in the hall. Mr Gatz spoke anxiously of the rain, and I asked the minister to wait for half an hour. But it wasn't any use. Nobody came.

♦

After the funeral we drove to the graveyard. Mr Gatz and the minister and me in one car, the servants and the postman from West Egg in another. As we walked towards the grave, I heard a car stop and then the sound of someone walking after us. I looked around. It was the man with the round glasses that I had found looking at Gatsby's books in the library during that first party.

I'd never seen him since then. I don't know how he knew about the funeral, or even his name.

'I couldn't get to the house,' he said.

'Neither could anybody else.'

'No! My God! They used to go there by the hundreds!' The rain poured down his thick glasses, and he took them off to watch Gatsby being lowered into the grave.

I tried to think about Gatsby then for a moment, but he was already too far away. I could only remember, without anger, that Daisy hadn't sent a message or a flower.

♦

I see now that this has been a story of the West after all – Tom and Gatsby, Daisy and Jordan and I, were all Westerners, and perhaps we possessed some lack in common which made us somehow uncomfortable with Eastern life.

After Gatsby's death the East was changed and spoilt for me. So in October I decided to come back home.

There was one thing to be done before I left, because I wanted to leave things in order. I saw Jordan Baker, and talked over and around what had happened to us together, and what had happened afterwards to me. She lay quite still, listening, in a big chair.

She was dressed to play golf, and I thought she looked like a good fashion photograph. When I had finished she told me that she was engaged to another man. I doubted that, though there were several men who would have been eager to marry her, but I pretended to be surprised.

'But you did throw me over,' said Jordan. 'You threw me over on the telephone. I don't care a bit about you now, but it was a new experience, and I felt strange for a while.'

I got up to say goodbye. We shook hands.

'Oh, and do you remember,' she added, 'a conversation we had once about driving a car? You said a bad driver was only safe until he met another bad driver. Well, I met another bad driver, didn't I? I made a wrong guess about you. I thought you were rather an honest person.'

Angry, and half in love with her, and enormously sorry, I turned away.

♦

One afternoon late in October I saw Tom Buchanan. He was walking ahead of me along Fifth Avenue. Suddenly he saw me and walked back, holding out his hand.

'What's the matter, Nick? Do you refuse to shake hands?'

'Yes. You know what I think of you. Tom,' I inquired, 'what did you say to Wilson that afternoon?'

He stared at me without a word, and I knew I had guessed right about those missing hours. I started to turn away, but he seized my arm.

'I told him the truth,' he said. 'He came to the door while we were getting ready to leave. I told the butler to say we weren't in, but he tried to force his way upstairs. He was crazy enough to kill me if I hadn't told him who owned the car. His hand was on a gun in his pocket—' He stopped suddenly. 'What if I did tell him? Gatsby deserved it. He ran over Myrtle like you'd run over a dog and never even stopped his car.'

There was nothing I could say. I couldn't tell him that it wasn't Gatsby who had run over Myrtle, but Daisy.

'And I had my share of suffering – look here, when I went to give up that flat and saw that dog food sitting there, I sat down and cried like a baby, it was terrible—'

I couldn't forgive him or like him, but I saw that what he had done was, to him, completely right. It was all very careless and confused. They were careless people, Tom and Daisy – they broke up things and creatures, and left other people to deal with the confusion, while they returned to their money, or their carelessness, or whatever it was that kept them together.

I shook hands with him; it seemed silly not to, for I felt suddenly as though I were talking to a child.

♦

Gatsby's house was still empty when I left – the grass on his lawn had grown as long as mine. I spent my Saturday nights in New York because those parties of his were with me so clearly that I could still hear the music and the laughter from his garden, and the cars going up and down his drive.

On the last night, with all my things packed and my car sold, I went over and looked at that enormous house once more. On the white steps some boy had written a dirty word, which stood out clearly in the moonlight. I rubbed it out with my shoe. Then I wandered down to the beach and sat on the sand.

Most of the big houses along the shore were closed now, and there were hardly any lights. As the moon rose higher the houses began to melt away until gradually I became conscious of the old island here, where the first Dutch sailors had landed – a fresh, green breast of the new world. The green trees that had made way for Gatsby's house had whispered once to those sailors on the shore; for a short magic moment they must have paused, face to face for the last time in history with a new world, the greatest of all human dreams.

And as I sat there thinking of the old, unknown world, I thought of Gatsby's wonder when he first picked out the green light at the end of Daisy's sea wall. He had come a long way to this blue lawn, and his dream must have seemed so close that he could hardly fail to seize it. He did not know that it was already behind him, somewhere back in that enormous darkness beyond the city, where the dark fields of the midwest rolled on under the night.

Gatsby believed in the green light, the magic promise of the future. He didn't realize that as we reach forward towards the dream, it moves ever further away from us. We press on, like boats against the current, and all the time we are carried back into the past.

ACTIVITIES

Chapters 1–2

Before you read

1 What do you think is the meaning of the phrase 'The American Dream'? What did American settlers hope for when they arrived in the United States in the eighteenth and nineteenth centuries?

2 Look at a map of the United States. Which states do you think are in the Middle West? How do you think they are culturally different from states on the East coast?

3 Look at the Word List at the back of this book. Discuss these questions.

   a Where can you see a *porch* and a *lawn*?

   b Which sport is more dangerous: *golf* or *polo*? Which one do you think is more exciting to watch? Why?

   c Would you prefer to be a *bond* salesperson, a *bootlegger* or a *butler*? What are some advantages and disadvantages of each job?

   d How common is *divorce* in your country? In what, if any, circumstances would you *approve* of *divorce*?

   e Would you expect people to drink *champagne* or *whisky* at an *engagement* party? Would a different drink be more common for this kind of occasion in your country?

   f Talk about a political scandal, in your own or another country, that you have read about.

While you read

4 What is the relationship between these pairs of people?

   a Nick and Daisy   ....

   b Daisy and Tom   ....

   c Jordan and Daisy   ....

   d Nick and Gatsby   ....

   e George and Myrtle   ....

   f Myrtle and Tom   ....

After you read

5 Why does:

   a Nick move to the East coast of America?

   b Nick know Jordan's face?

   c Tom visit a garage?

   d Tom hit Myrtle?

6 What impression does Nick Carraway give you of the following people and places?

   a The Middle West of the United States after World War I

   b West Egg and East Egg

   c His rented house in West Egg

   d Tom Buchanan

   e Daisy Buchanan

   f Tom and Daisy's house in East Egg

   g Miss Jordan Baker

   h Mr George Wilson

   i Mrs Myrtle Wilson

Chapters 3–4

Before you read

7 What did Nick see when he watched Gatsby in his garden late at night? What explanation might there be for Gatsby's behaviour?

8 Think of the most amazing party you have ever attended. What made it so remarkable?

While you read

9 Are these sentences true (T) or false (F)?

   a An invitation is not necessary to get into one of Jay Gatsby's parties. .....

   b Gatsby greets Nick when he arrives and introduces him to several other guests. .....

   c Jordan Baker lost a recent golf match. .....

   d The party guests don't actually seem to know their host very well. .....

e Gatsby is the fat, middle-aged man in the library.   .....

f Gatsby's smile gives Nick a positive impression of his
character.   .....

g Gatsby always joins in the fun at his parties.   .....

h Jordan Baker insists on honesty from herself and her
friends.   .....

10 Circle the correct answer.

a Jay Gatsby's car is *big and expensive / small and economical.*

b Nick Carraway's first impression of Gatsby is that he is *very
important / rather ordinary.*

c A war decoration and a photo at Oxford University make Nick
believe / doubt Gatsby's extraordinary stories.

d Gatsby has a habit of driving *extremely slowly / very fast.*

e At lunch with Gatsby, Nick gets the impression that Meyer
Wolfshiem is *an honest businessman / a clever criminal.*

f At the same lunch, Gatsby is *upset / delighted* to meet Tom
Buchanan.

g On the night before her wedding, a letter makes Daisy feel
unsure / confident about marrying Tom.

h Jay Gatsby moves to West Egg because he wants to *meet
Jordan Baker / be near Daisy Buchanan.*

After you read

11 What effect does alcohol have on these people?

a the guests at Gatsby's parties (including the fat, middle-aged
man in the library)

b Nick Carraway

c Jay Gatsby

d Daisy Buchanan

12 In your opinion, how are these people dishonest about these
subjects?

a Jordan Baker, about a borrowed car and about winning at golf

b Nick Carraway, about his relationship with a girl back home

   c Jay Gatsby, about his reasons for making friends with Jordan and Nick, his family background and his wealth, his education and his war record

   d Meyer Wolfshiem, about his part in a sports scandal in 1919

   e Daisy, about her happiness at marrying Tom Buchanan

   f Tom Buchanan, about his role as a husband

13 Who makes these remarks and why?

   a 'I'm afraid I'm not a very good host.'

   b 'I hate careless people. That's why I like you.'

   c 'Know you next time, Mr Gatsby. Excuse *me*!'

   d 'Say: "Daisy's changed her mind!"'

   e 'You just have to invite her to tea.'

Chapters 5–6

14 American school children use the word HOMES to remember the names of the five Great Lakes between the US and Canada. H is for Lake Huron. Find out what O, M, E and S are for.

15 Which of these relationships do you think will be most important to the story? Why?

   a Daisy and Tom Buchanan

   b Myrtle Wilson and Tom Buchanan

   c Daisy Buchanan and Jay Gatsby

   d Jordan Baker and Nick Carraway

While you read

16 Complete these sentences. Write one word in each space.

   a When Nick returns home, Jay Gatsby suggests a ....

   b Then Gatsby offers Nick ....

   c Nick invites Daisy and Gatsby to .... at his house.

   d Then Gatsby shows Daisy his own ....

   e On more than one occasion, the visit makes Daisy ....

   f Nick only learns the truth about Gatsby's .... much later.

   g Tom Buchanan is .... that Gatsby has met his wife.

   h Both Tom and Daisy attend a .... at Gatsby's house.

17 Match these, from Gatsby's real background, with the descriptions.

a James Gatz

b North Dakota

c farming

d seventeen

e Lake Superior

f mines

g Ella Kaye

h Tuomalee

i five

j women and drink

1) the place where Gatsby first saw Dan Cody

2) Dan Cody's weaknesses

3) Dan Cody's sailboat

4) Gatsby's real name

5) what made Dan Cody rich

6) the years that Gatsby spent with Dan Cody

7) Gatsby's parents' profession

8) a journalist who gets Cody's money

9) the age when James Gatz changed his name

10) the state the Gatzes live in

18 How do these people feel?

a Nick, when Gatsby offers him work

b Gatsby, during the tea party at Nick's house

c Mr Sloane, when he meets Jay Gatsby

d Tom, after his first visit to Gatsby's house

e Daisy, at Gatsby's party

f Gatsby, after the party

19 Work in pairs. Act out one of these conversations between Daisy and Gatsby.

a At their first meeting at Nick's house when Nick goes out into the garden and leaves the couple alone for the first time in almost five years.

b When they escape from the party and sit on Nick's steps while Nick keeps watch in the garden.

Chapters 7–8

Before you read

20 In your opinion, is it important for a husband and wife or for two friends to be faithful to each other? What usually happens when a person is unfaithful to a friend or partner?

21 Do you think Gatsby's dream of a life with Daisy will come true? Give reasons for your answer.

While you read

22 Who is it? Write **T** for Tom Buchanan or **J** for Jay Gatsby.

a He hires new servants.   .....

b He talks on the telephone about selling his car.   .....

c He is surprised by Pammy Buchanan.   .....

d He exchanges romantic looks with Daisy.   .....

e He doesn't want to drive his own car into town.   .....

f He stops at Wilson's garage for gas.   .....

g He was in Oxford for five months in 1919.   .....

h He admits that he has been unfaithful to Daisy.   .....

i He believes that Daisy has never loved her husband.   .....

j He goes back to Long Island in his own car with Daisy.   .....

23 Complete this report about the car accident in Chapter 8.

a	Witness's name:	....
b	Time of accident:	....
c	Direction the car was heading:	....
d	Place of accident:	....
e	Name of dead person:	....
f	Cause of accident:	....
g	Description of car:	....
h	Driver:	....

After you read

24 How does Tom Buchanan discover his wife's feelings for Gatsby?

25 Discuss jealousy. What causes Tom Buchanan, Gatsby, Mr Wilson and Myrtle Wilson to feel jealous? How do feelings of jealousy destroy feelings of love?

26 Tell the story of Myrtle's death from the point of view of these people. In each case, say how you feel.

    a her husband

    b Daisy

    c Tom

Chapters 9–10

Before you read

27 Do you think Daisy will leave Tom for Gatsby? What reasons are there for her to stay or to leave?

28 Look at the headings for the last two chapters and say what you think will happen.

    a 'Murder'   Who will kill whom? Why?

    b 'Saying goodbye'   Who will say goodbye to whom? Why?

While you read

29 Put Nick's actions on the day after Myrtle Wilson dies in the correct order, 1–6.

    a He finds Gatsby's body in his pool. .....

    b He advises Gatsby to go away. .....

    c He talks to Jordan Baker on the phone. .....

    d He sees Mr Wilson's dead body. .....

    e He falls asleep at his desk in the city. .....

    f He eats breakfast with Gatsby. .....

30 Write the name of the character. Who:

    a protects her sister's good name? ....

    b has to answer all the questions about his dead friend? ....

    c leave East Egg without saying goodbye to anyone? .... and ....

d has a problem about stolen bonds? ....

e isn't surprised by death but is very
proud of his son's wealth? ....

f is more interested in tennis shoes than
in a friend's death? ....

g got Gatsby started in money-making
businesses? ....

h tells Nick that she is engaged? ....

i tells Mr Wilson that Jay Gatsby killed
his wife? ....

After you read

31 Discuss why Nick takes so much trouble over gatsby's funeral, who attends, and how Nick feels about it.

32 At the end of the story, how does Nick feel about:

a Jordan?

b Daisy and Tom?

33 Discuss why Nick makes a connection between the first Dutch sailors who landed on the east coast of the United States and Jay Gatsby.

Writing

34 You are a guest at one of Jay Gatsby's really big parties. Write a letter to your parents in a small town in the Middle West and describe this extraordinary experience.

35 You are Jordan Baker. Write a page in your diary about your new boyfriend, Nick Carraway.

36 Write a newspaper report about the deaths of Gatsby and George Wilson.

37 Explain how Nick's relationship with Gatsby develops through the story.

38 Describe the character of either Tom or Daisy Buchanan. How sympathetic do you feel about his or her troubles?

39 Tell the story of Gatsby's life. Which parts of his background are never fully explained?

40 Write a telephone conversation between Nick Carraway and his parents. Nick has phoned to say that he is returning home. His parents want to know his reasons and his plans for the future.

41 Explain why so many people attend Gatsby's parties and so few attend his funeral.

42 Sometimes the United States is described as a classless society, meaning that there are no social divisions which separate people. Does this book support this idea or not? Explain your position.

43 Write a reader's report on the book. Tell the story in two or three paragraphs and then explain why you did or did not enjoy it.

WORD LIST

approve (v) to believe that someone or something is acceptable

ash (n) the soft grey powder that is left after something has been burned

astonished (adj) very surprised

bay (n) a part of a coastline where the land curves in

bond (n) a certificate from a government or company showing that you have lent them money

bootlegger (n) someone who makes and sells products illegally

butler (n) the most important male servant in a big house

champagne (n) a French wine that is often drunk on special occasions

civilized (adj) with highly developed laws and social customs

delicately (adv) carefully, so that no offence is given

divorce (n) the legal ending of a marriage

drugstore (n) a shop in the US where you can buy medicines and other goods and get drinks and snacks

engaged (adj) having agreed to marry someone

golf (n) a game in which you try to hit a small white ball into holes in the ground

groan (v) to make a long, deep sound, usually because you are in pain

insist (v) to say something firmly

lawn (n) an area of grass that is kept cut short

miserable (adj) not at all good; unhappy

muscle (n) one of the pieces of flesh that join your bones together and make your body move

polo (n) a game played on horses by two teams who hit a small ball with long, wooden sticks

porch (n) an entrance covered by a roof, built onto a house

scandal (n) a situation or event that people think is immoral or shocking

scorn (n) an opinion that someone or something is stupid or worthless

sideline (n) something that you do to earn money in addition to your regular job

silk (n) soft, fine cloth made from a substance produced by a kind of small animal

standard (n) an idea of what is good or normal, used to compare things

tremble (v) to shake because you are worried, afraid or excited

unfold (v) to show something gradually

unit (n) a group of people who are part of a larger group

whisky (n) a strong alcoholic drink made from grain

Rebecca
Daphne du Maurier

After the death of his beautiful wife, Rebecca, Maxim de Winter goes to Monte Carlo to forget the past. There he marries a quiet young woman and takes her back to Manderley, his lovely country home. But the memory of Rebecca casts a dark shadow on the new marriage. Then the discovery of a sunken boat shatters the new Mrs de Winter's dream of a happy life.

Four Weddings and a Funeral
Richard Curtis

It's a Saturday morning, and Charles is still asleep. He should be on his way to Angus and Laura's wedding! Charles is always late, and he is always going to other people's weddings. He's worried that he will never find the right woman to marry. Then he meets Carrie and he wants to be with her very much . . .

Taste and Other Tales
Roald Dahl

In this collection of Roald Dahl's finest stories we meet some quite ordinary people who behave in extraordinary ways. There is a man who is sure he can hear plants scream and the wife who discovers a perfect way to get rid of her husband. And there's a woman who finds an unusual use for a leg of lamb . . .

There are hundreds of Penguin Readers to choose from – world classics, film adaptations, modern-day crime and adventure, short stories, biographies, American classics, non-fiction, plays ...

For a complete list of all Penguin Readers titles, please contact your local Pearson Longman office or visit our website.

www.penguinreaders.com

Jane Eyre
Charlotte Brontë

Jane Eyre, a poor orphan, grows up in misery until she becomes the governess in the house of wealthy Mr Rochester and falls in love. But mysterious events take place in the house at night, and Mr Rochester appears to be hiding a terrible secret. Can Jane even hope for happiness?

Pride and Prejudice
Jane Austen

Jane and Elizabeth Bennet are the oldest of five sisters in need of husbands, but it isn't easy to find the right man. Are Mr Bingley, Mr Darcy and Mr Wickham all that they seem? Will pride and prejudice ever be defeated in the search for true love?

Wuthering Heights
Emily Brontë

On the wild and lonely Yorkshire moors, a tragic story unfolds as Catherine Earnshaw and Heathcliff fall in love. But it is a dangerous love, filled with unhappiness and suffering. When Catherine finally breaks Heathcliff's heart, Heathcliff decides to break everyone else's and plans a terrible revenge.

There are hundreds of Penguin Readers to choose from – world classics, film adaptations, modern-day crime and adventure, short stories, biographies, American classics, non-fiction, plays ...

For a complete list of all Penguin Readers titles, please contact your local Pearson Longman office or visit our website.

Longman Dictionaries

Express yourself with confidence!

PEARSON
Longman

Longman has led the way in ELT dictionaries since 1935. We constantly talk to students and teachers around the world to find out what they need from a learner's dictionary.

Why choose a Longman dictionary?

Easy to understand

Longman invented the Defining Vocabulary – 2000 of the most common words which are used to write the definitions in our dictionaries. So Longman definitions are always clear and easy to understand.

Real, natural English

All Longman dictionaries contain natural examples taken from real-life that help explain the meaning of a word and show you how to use it in context.

Avoid common mistakes

Longman dictionaries are written specially for learners, and we make sure that you get all the help you need to avoid common mistakes. We analyse typical learners' mistakes and include notes on how to avoid them.

Innovative CD-ROMs

Longman are leaders in dictionary CD-ROM innovation. Did you know that a dictionary CD-ROM includes features to help improve your pronunciation, help you practice for exams and improve your writing skills?

For details of all Longman dictionaries, and to choose the one that's right for you, visit our website:

www.longman.com/dictionaries